# Sleepwalkers on a Picnic

(Prose Poems)

## Zvonko Karanović

Translated from the Serbian with an afterword by
Biljana D. Obradović

DIÁLOGOS
BOOKS
New Orleans
Diálogosbooks.com

*Sleepwalkers on a Picnic (Prose Poems)*
An English translation of *Mesečari na izletu (Pesme u prozi)*.
by Zvonko Karanović
Translated with an afterword by Biljana D. Obradović
Copyright © 2020 Biljana D. Obradović and Diálogos Books.
Serbian original copyright © Zvonko Karanović.

Cover Art: "Bus Full of Sleepwalkers" by Simon Kastelic © 2019
.
All rights reserved. No part of this work may be reproduced
in any form without the express written permission
of the copyright holders and Diálogos Books.

Printed in the U.S.A.
First Printing
10 9 8 7 6 5 4 3 2 1    19 20 21 22 23 24

Book design: Bill Lavender

Library of Congress Control Number:  2019947886
Karanović, Zvonko
*Sleepwalkers on a Picnic (Prose Poems)* / Zvonko Karanović;
with Biljana D. Obradović (translator)
p. cm.
ISBN: 978-1-944884-70-3

Publication of this book is made possible in part by a generous grant from the Serbian Ministry of Culture, Belgrade.

# Acknowledgements

The poem "Decisiveness of Middle Age" was previously published in a slightly different form in *Cat Painters: An Anthology of Contemporary Serbian Poetry*. Eds. Biljana D. Obradović and Dubravka Djurić. Diálogos, 2016. Pp. 219-220, and in *World Literature Today*, May 2013. Printed with permission of the translator and author.

Parts of the Introduction with Zvonko Karanović have appeared in my interview with him in *World Literature Today* online: Interview for *WLT* with Biljana D. Obradović, "Rebel with a Cause in Serbia: A Conversation with Zvonko Karanović." Oct 2012. Read full text at http://www.worldliteraturetoday.org/2013/may/rebel-cause-serbia-conversation-zvonko-karanovic-biljana-d-obradovic#.UgjOFn__SMU Printed with permission of the translator and author.

Biljana would like to thank the following for their help in making this book possible: Xavier University of Louisiana's Department of English without whose support my trips to Serbia during the summers to work on these translations would have been more difficult; my Deans, Dr. Anil Kukreja and Dr. Camellia Okpodu, and my Division Chair, Dr. Steven Salm, thanks for the support for summer teaching; Zvonko Karanović, the author of these amazing poems, for all your suggestions in Belgrade and your friendship; to Simon Kastelic for your cover art, I hope to meet you some day; John Gery, my husband, who has edited a lot of this with love and care, your language ability amazes me; Tim Skeen, comrade, thanks for proofing, and blurbing; Julie Kane, thanks for being there when needed most, and blurbing; Dubravka Djurić, always there, and for blurbing; Elza Ivović Holt, for your decades of friendship, everlasting, always there to help; to Vesna Kilibarda, my closest friend, without you, I would not be sane; to Bill Lavender, my publisher, for your willingness to publish this and for your patience; to Petar, my son, I live for you.

Finally I especially would like to thank Mr. Mladen Vesković, senior advisor, and Chief of the Department for International Cooperation, the Sector for International Cooperation, European Integration and Projects of the Republic of Serbia for the translation grant.

The translations in this poetry collection have been made possible by a generous grant from the Ministry of Culture and Information of the Republic of Serbia.

# Mesečari na izletu

| | |
|---|---|
| U hotelskoj sobi | 14 |
| Zapis iz kartonske crkve | 18 |
| Iznenadni događaji u muzeju uspomena | 22 |
| O kiši i kraju ljubavi | 24 |
| Odlazak u novi um | 28 |
| Bilo je proleće i ljubav je uzimala nov zamah | 30 |
| Komesar | 32 |
| Preobražaj | 36 |
| Avioni budućnosti | 38 |
| Napušten od svetova | 42 |
| O mladosti i stvarima koje bi trebalo da su istinite | 46 |
| Izlet | 48 |
| Dok su se zveri prikradale | 52 |
| O otkriću dva izumrla sveta | 54 |
| Podignute zavese | 56 |
| U bespućima poezije | 60 |
| Popodne jednog Fauna | 66 |
| Slučaj službenika reklamne agencije | 70 |
| Književnost i nasilje | 74 |
| Sirotica | 76 |
| Borba Titana | 80 |
| Sudar mišljenja u različitim vremenskim zonama | 82 |
| Hronika najavljenog nestanka | 84 |
| Dugokose muzičke sirene | 86 |
| Poezija za svačiji dom | 88 |
| Odlučnost srednjih godina | 90 |
| Bekstvo nakon kratke molitve | 92 |
| Udarac za udarcem | 96 |
| Dartovski čovek | 98 |
| Epifanija, mala demonstracija moći | 102 |
| Spiritualni život | 104 |

# Sleepwalkers on a Picnic

| | |
|---|---|
| In a Hotel Room | 15 |
| Notes from a Cardboard Church | 19 |
| Sudden Events in the Museum of Memories | 23 |
| About Rain and the End of Love | 25 |
| Departure for a New Mind | 29 |
| In Spring with Love in Full Swing | 31 |
| Commissar | 33 |
| Metamorphosis | 37 |
| Airplanes of the Future | 39 |
| Abandoned by Worlds | 43 |
| About Youth and Things That Should Be Truthful | 47 |
| Picnic | 49 |
| While the Beasts Crept in | 53 |
| Upon Discovering Two Lost Worlds | 55 |
| Lifted Curtains | 57 |
| In the Wilderness of Poetry | 61 |
| Afternoon of a Faun | 67 |
| The Case of an Advertising Agency Employee | 71 |
| Literature and Violence | 75 |
| A Waif | 77 |
| The Battle of the Titans | 81 |
| Clash of Opinions in Different Time Zones | 83 |
| Chronicle of a Preset Disappearance | 85 |
| Long-Haired Musical Mermaids | 87 |
| Poetry for Everyone's Home | 89 |
| Decisiveness of Middle Age | 91 |
| Escape after a Short Prayer | 93 |
| Blow after Blow | 97 |
| Dartian Man | 99 |
| Epiphany, a Small Demonstration of Power | 103 |
| Spiritual Life | 105 |

O uticaju razređenog vazduha na povređeno samoljublje 106
Uskrsnuća-nestajanja 110
Tajanstvena plavuša 112
Misterije organizma 116
Nesigurnosti 120
Učiteljevim stopama 124
Strujanje misli u kupatilu 126
Edip, na rubu ponora 128
Jedan život, jedna karijera 130
Demoni u bordelu 134

| | |
|---|---|
| About the Influence of Diluted Air on the Injured Self | 107 |
| Resurrections-Disappearances | 111 |
| The Mysterious Blonde | 113 |
| Mysteries of the Organism | 117 |
| Uncertainties | 121 |
| In the Teacher's Footsteps | 125 |
| The Streaming of Thoughts in the Bathroom | 127 |
| Oedipus, on the Brink of an Abyss | 129 |
| One Life, One Career | 133 |
| Demons in the Brothel | 137 |
| | |
| Afterword | 141 |
| Notes | 154 |
| About the Author | 157 |
| About the Translator | 159 |
| About the Artist | 161 |

**Mesečari na izletu**

# Sleepwalkers on a Picnic

Tražio sam pogledom znakove grada. Divlji zec je pretrčao put, a još dalje napred neki policajac se naslanjao na motocikl. Instinktivno sam usporio, a potom zaustavio auto. „Dobro jutro, gospodine", rekao sam. „Čini mi se da sam pogrešno skrenuo. Možete li mi reći gde sam? " „Ne baš", odgovorio je. „Izgleda da je ovo novo područje."

—Džejms Tejt, *U nelagodi zbog zvukova nekih životinja što lutaju noću*

I looked around for signs of the city. A jack-rabbit scurried across the road, and up ahead a policeman was leaning against his motorcycle. I slowed down instinctively, and then pulled over to stop. "Good morning, officer," I said. "I seem to have taken a wrong turn. Could you tell me where I am?" "Not exactly," he said. "This seems to be a new area."

—James Tate, *Uneasy about the Sounds of Some Night-Wandering Animal*

## U hotelskoj sobi

Sedeo je na krevetu u hotelskoj sobi, samo u belim boksericama koje su mu dopirale skoro do kolena.
Razgovarao je telefonom s majkom.
Njegova majka bila je odavno mrtva.
Glas iz slušalice samo je ličio na glas njegove majke.
„Dubina detalja je presudna u pisanju", neko je govorio s druge strane.
Velika gola žena, širokih ramena i masivnih butina, igrala je iza njega.
Sporo se izvijala uz ritam elektronske muzike koja je tiho dopirala iz zvučnika raspoređenih po uglovima sobe.
Potom je čuo:
„Izbegavaš ženske likove, fasciniran si mašinama... Tvoj otac je bio na putu kada sam te rodila... "
S izrazom dosade na licu, žena iza njegovih leđa je prišla i prekinula vezu.
„Ne treba pisati o smrti, živimo u kulturi hepiendinga", rekla je metalnim, robotskim glasom.
Zažmurio je.
Našao se u luksuznom apartmanu punom striptizeta.
Telefon je zvonio.
Dugo mu je bilo potrebno da ispruži ruku i podigne slušalicu.
„Nedostatak ograničenja je neprijatelj umetnosti... ", ponovo je začuo majčin glas.
Nije više slušao.
Gledao je tri plavuše na visokim potpeticama kako mu prilaze i prave krug oko njega.

## In a Hotel Room

He was sitting on the bed in a hotel room, wearing only in his white boxers reaching down almost to his knees.

He was talking on the phone with his mother.

His mother had been dead a long time.

The voice coming from the receiver only resembled his mother's.

"The depth of details is key in writing," someone said from the other end.

A large, naked woman, with broad shoulders and massive thighs, danced behind him.

She was slowly writhing to the rhythm of the electronic music coming quietly through speakers arranged neatly around the corners of the room.

Then he heard:

"Fascinated by machines, you are avoiding female characters... When I gave birth to you, your father was away on business..."

With an expression of boredom, the woman behind him came closer and disconnected the phone line.

"One shouldn't be writing about death; we live in a culture of happy endings," she said in a metalic, robotic voice.

He closed his eyes.

He found himself in a luxury apartment full of strippers.

The phone rang.

It took him a long time to reach out and lift the receiver.

"The lack of boundaries is the enemy of art...," he heard his mother's voice say, again.

He stopped listening.

He watched three blondes in high heels approach and then encircle him.

Dve su iščupale telefonski kabl, obmotale ga oko njegovog vrata i počele da ga dave.

Treća mu je ogromnim silikonskim grudima pritiskala lice ne dozvoljavajući mu da diše.

Dobio je snažnu erekciju.

Nije ni pokušao da se odbrani, čak im je pomagao u gušenju.

Zatezao je kabl oko svog vrata najjače moguće, ali imao je utisak da bezuspešno zateže dečiji lastiš, mlitavu želatinsku traku.

Two of them pulled the phone cable out of the wall, tied it around his neck and began to squeeze.

The third sqashed his face with her enormous, silicone breasts, suffocating him.

He got a strong erection.

He didn't even try to defend himself, but instead helped them tighten the cord.

He tightened it around his neck as much as he could, but he had the sense he was tightening a kid's elastic band, to no effect, a limp gelatin band.

## Zapis iz kartonske crkve

Samo u početku dolazile su mu vizije pune vatre i pepela.

Kasnije su ih zamenile sasvim obične, poput one da more uranja u sunce, ili kako u vodi dubokoj metar vozi bicikl, ili kako mislima komanduje pticama.

Nije to bilo ništa čudno.

Zadatak mu je i bio da „ima vizije", zabeleži ih, i s vremena na vreme pošalje onima koje to uopšte ne zanima.

Iako se nije smatrao ni prorokom ni propovednikom, sagradio je crkvu na olupanom uličnom kontejneru.

U crkvu, kartonsku kutiju požutelu od kiše i sunca, primio je šugavo mače.

Pravilo mu je društvo dok je, uglavnom posle ponoći, osvetljen svetlošću sveće pisao sebi pisma.

Dani su mu tekli mirno sve do velikog incidenta čiji je povod bila rečenica:

*Kada ostanemo sami moramo se usredsrediti na izgled.*

Čim je stavio tačku na svoju misao prolomilo se nebo.

Zakreštale su svrake na gubilištu, zacijukali slepi miševi savesti.

Iz mračnih dubina ošinuo ga je unutrašnji glas:

„Spoljašnost je iluzija! Sve što postoji je unutra!"

Uplašen, brzo je zapisivao:

*Način opstanka... Negiranje površnosti... Život ispod površine...*

Setio se kako to piše samome sebi i da nema potrebe za pravdanjem, pa je odložio olovku.

## Notes from a Cardboard Church

Only in the beginning did the visions come to him, full of fire and ashes.

Later they were replaced by others that seemed ordinary, like those in which the sea rises into the sun, or how in water a meter deep, he is riding a bicycle, or how he commands birds with his thoughts.

They weren't strange at all.

His job was to "have visions," to write them down, and from time to time to deliver them to those who didn't care about them anyway.

Even though he considered himself neither a prophet nor a preacher, still, he built a church on a beat-up dumpster.

Into the church, a cardboard box yellowed from rain and sunlight, he welcomed a mangy kitten.

It kept him company, while after midnight, mostly by candlelight, he wrote letters to himself.

Days passed peacefully until the big incident occurred, caused by this sentence:

*When we are left alone we must concentrate on our image.*

As soon as he put down a period, the thunderstorm began.

Magpies started to screech loudly on the gallows, while the bats of conscience peeped in from the rafters.

From out of the depths of darkness an inner voice began to whip him,

"Appearance is an illusion! Everything that exists is inside!"

Frightened, he wrote quickly,

*The mode of existence... Negating superficiality... Life beneath the surface...*

Then, he remembered he was writing only to himself with no need to defend himself, so he put down his pencil.

Šugavo mače u uglu podiglo je šapu.

Zakačena kao bedž na njegovim grudima, majušna neonska reklama koka-kole zatreperila je u mraku, i on je najzad shvatio da je tu iz sasvim pogrešnih razloga.

In the corner the mangy kitten raised its paw.

Attached to his chest as if a badge, the tiny, neon Coca-Cola sign flickered in the darkness, until he finally realized that he was there for completely the wrong reasons.

## Iznenadni događaji u muzeju uspomena

Sedeo je u jeftinoj fotelji od veštačke kože i dugo zurio u natpis na zidu:
*Čovek se mora potruditi da bi ga shvatili ozbiljno!*
Pogled mu je skliznuo ka vitrini na kojoj su stajali prašnjavi gramofon, odavno van upotrebe, uramljena fotografija nasmejane devojke i zbirka pesama *Boravak u paklu*.
Polako je ustao i otišao u kuhinju.
Vratio se s malom sekirom.
Najpre je smrvio ram.
Potom je snažnim udarcem zdrobio plastični poklopac gramofona, bacio gramofon na pod i divljački ga izgazio.
Nekoliko trenutaka gledao je lom pred sobom i uzeo knjigu s vitrine.
Nije želeo da je odmah rastrgne na komade.
Vratio se u fotelju i s uživanjem, sadistički, cepao stranicu po stranicu povremeno se zaustavljajući kako bi nasumice pročitao po koji stih.
Kad su mu u rukama ostale samo korice, zadovoljno je pogledao u natpis na zidu.
Napolju se mrak zgušnjavao u potmulo režanje.
Unutra su razbacane stvari činile nov, potpuno svež i neočekivan poredak.

## Sudden Events in the Museum of Memories

Sitting in a cheap, faux leather armchair, he stared at the sign on the wall for a long time:
*Men must try harder in order to be taken more seriously!*
His eyes then fell on a wooden commode with a dusty, broken record player on it, lacking a needle, unused for some time, with a framed photograph of a smiling girl, and a collection of poems, *A Season in Hell*.
Eventually he rose and went to the kitchen.
He returned with a small hatchet.
First he hacked the frame.
Then with a strong blow, he flattened the plastic cover of the record player, threw the machine on the floor, and stomped on it wildly.
For a few moments he stared at the debris in front of him and grabbed the book from the case.
He didn't want to tear it apart immediately.
He went back to the armchair, where joyfully, sadistically, he ripped it page by page, stopping from time to time so he might read a random line or two.
When he held only the covers in his hands, he looked up at the sign on the wall, satisfied.
Outside the darkness thickened into a dull growl.
Inside the scattered mess arranged itself into a new, fresh and quite surprising order!

## O kiši i kraju ljubavi

S neprozirnog neba visili su tamni, otežali oblaci nalik prljavim krpama.
Stajao je i čekao, gledajući nazmenično u nebo, pa na sat.
Žurilo mu se.
U haustoru je upravo ubio junaka jednog Godarovog filma.
Napokon, njen automobil se zaustavio.
Otvorio je vrata i hitro šmugnuo u vozilo.
Ćutao je.
Ruke su mu se tresle.
Gledao je u njena kolena koja su se naizmenično podizala i spuštala.
U njena stopala koja su naizmenično pristiskala pedale.
U njene duge prste kojima je stezala volan.
U pramen njene kose zadenut iza uha.
U njen dečji profil.
Pokušao je da pronađe neku drugu muziku na radiju.
Bio je dan žalosti i sve stanice emitovale su klasiku.
Izašli su iz grada, skrenuli s glavnog puta i zaustavili se nadomak šumice.
Isključio je radio.
Želeo je da joj ispriča kako je upravo ubio njenog muža, zbog nje, zbog njih.
Želeo je sve da joj ispriča, ali kao da nije imao dovoljno vazduha.
Okrenula se k njemu i nežno ga pomilovala po kosi.
Gledao je u crno, preteće nebo, ne pomerajući

## About Rain and the End of Love

From the murky sky, heavy clouds hung like dirty rags.

He stood and waited, looking at the sky, then intermittently at his watch.

He was in a big hurry.

In the foyer he had just killed the hero of a Godard movie.

Finally, her car arrived.

He opened the door and quickly disappeared into the shotgun seat.

He was silent.

His hands were trembling.

He looked at her knees which she kept raising then lowering, first one, then the other.

At her feet, with which she intermittently pushed the pedals back and forth.

At her long fingers, with which she gripped the steering wheel tightly.

At her one strand of hair tucked behind her ear.

At her child-like profile.

He tried to find some alternative music on the radio.

But it was a day of mourning, so all radio stations played only classical music.

They left the city, left the main road and stopped near a little forest.

He turned off the radio.

He wanted to tell her that he had just murdered her husband because of her, because of them.

He wanted to tell her everything, but he felt he was gasping for air.

She turned toward him and gently caressed his hair.

He looked at the dark, threatening sky without moving his

glavu.

U daljini munja je zaparala horizont.

Prolomio se strahovit prasak i krupne kapi kiše počele su da zasipaju stakla.

head.

In the distance lightning flashed intermittendly on the horizon.

A loud boom rang out, shaking the air, as huge raindrops began to splatter on the windshield.

## Odlazak u novi um

Trudio se da ne razmišlja o prošlosti, ali o prošlosti je jedino razmišljao.

Napolju su ljudi postajali sve nervozniji.

Raširene noge ulica povijale su se pred jakobinskim pokličima gnevnih.

Prikaze su užurbano hodale i gurale prste u svako otvoreno oko.

Sklonio se u knjigu i tamo upoznao devojku koja je jezikom pesak pretvarala u zlato.

Nalik skupocenoj striptizeti igrala je za njega i nije tražila da s njom provede ostatak života.

Stajao je obasjan novim prolećem.

Bradati i moćni bardovi iskrsavali su na obzorju.

Jedan dečak skakutao je po rečenicama bez namere da ga pozdravi.

## Departure for a New Mind

Athough he was trying not to think about the past, it was all he thought about.

People outside were becoming more nervous.

The bent legs of the streets were spreading out in front of the Jacobean calls of the angry mob.

Apparitions were walking around hastily, sticking their fingers into each open eye.

He hid himself in a book where he met a girl who with her tongue could turn sand into gold.

As if an expensive stripper, she danced for him without asking him to spend the rest of his life with her.

He stood up, illuminated by the new spring.

Bearded and powerful bards popped up along the horizon.

A boy was splashing on sentences with no intention of ever saying hello to him.

## Bilo je proleće i ljubav je uzimala nov zamah

Mučen nesanicom, noću bi se satima prevrtao po krevetu.

Tek pred svitanje, umor bi ga savladao i odvlačio u snove, čudne snove koji kao da nisu bili njegovi.

Tako se jednom obreo u koncentracionom logoru kao plavokosa kuhinjska radnica.

Sledeći put bio je kamena urna namenjena čuvanju pepela nastradalih ljubavnika.

Potom je postao psihijatrijski bolesnik kolutavih očiju koji svira harmoniku na ulazu u groblje.

Vodio je monoton samački život.

Jedva je čekao da zaspi kako bi mu se dogodilo nešto neobično.

Jednom prilikom našao se u nepoznatom gradu.

Stajao je ispred neke škole.

Iznenada je začuo psovke, uzvike, pretnje.

Okrenuo se i video rulju kako juri k njemu.

Izobličena lica žena i muškaraca brzo su mu se približavala.

Želeo je da se skloni, pobegne nekud, ali dete u njegovom naručju smetalo mu je da potrči.

Uzalud se trudio da se probudi dok su mu po glavi pljuštali udarci, dok se prisećao šta je zapravo želeo s tim detetom.

## In Spring with Love in Full Swing

    Suffering from insomnia, he would spend nights rolling over in bed.

    Just before dawn, exhaustion would overtake him and drag him into dreams, strange dreams as if they belonged to someone else.

    In one of them, he ended up in a concentration camp as a blonde kitchen maid.

    Next as a stone urn meant for holding the ashes of deceased lovers.

    Then a psychiatric patient with bulging eyes who played the accordion at the cemetery gate.

    In fact, he lead a monotonous life like a hermit.

    He couldn't wait to fall asleep so that something unusual might happen to him.

    One time he found himself in an unfamiliar city.

    He was standing in front of a some sort of school.

    Suddenly he heard curses, shouts, threats.

    He turned around to see a mob rushing towards him.

    The contorted faces of women and men were quickly coming at him. . .

    He wanted to find a shelter to get away somewhere, but the child in his arms weighed him down.

    While their punches were smashing his head, in vain he tried to wake up, as he tried to remember what exactly it was he really wanted to do with that child.

# Komesar

Sa zanimanjem je odgledao film o životu političkog komesara nekakve neimenovane ekstremističke organizacije.
U filmu, Komesar je klečao pred raspećem:

„Bože, zašto sam tako slab?", ridao je. „Zašto mi ne pokažeš put?..."
Obrisao je suze, obukao kožni mantil, za pojas zadenuo revolver i krenuo u redakciju.
Spadale su mu mrežaste čarape ispod kožnih pantalona dok je prkosio pretnjama i klevetama nezadovoljnih čitalaca.
Spadala mu je mrežica za kosu ispod kožne kape dok je jurcao od svoje kancelarije do štamparije.
Njegovi zadaci bili su jednostavni:
Cenzura nepodobnih!
Zastrašivanje neodlučnih!
Likvidacija neposlušnih!
Potom sve iznova: jutrom klečanje pred raspećem, suze, molitve, neuslišene molitve.
I ponovo, smrknuto lice na izlasku iz kuće i odlazak na radno mesto, u orman s natpisom: *Isus je upravo napustio grad.*

Razmišljao je o odgledanom filmu.
Pitao se da li je seksualna frustriranost glavnog junaka uzrok njegovog ideološkog fanatizma.
Pitao se i šta znači natpis: *Isus je upravo napustio grad.*
Verovatno je i to ukazivalo na nešto.
Padalo je veče, približavalo se vreme izlaska.

# Commissar

With great interest, he watched an entire film on the life of a political commissar of some unnamed extremist party.

In the film, the commissar knelt before the crucifixion:

"God, why am I so weak?" he sobbed. "Why don't you show me the way?"

He wiped his tears, put on his long leather coat, stuck a gun in his holster and went to the press office.

His fishnet stockings were slipping under his leather pants while he was rejecting the insults from unsatisfied readers.

His hair net came loose under his leather cap while he rushed from his office to the printer's.

His duties were simple:

Censor the unsuitable!

Scare away the indecisive!

Liquidate the disobedient!

And then all over again: in the mornings on his knees in front of the crucifixion, tears, prayers, and hindered prayers.

And once again, a grim face before leaving the house to go to the office, into an armoire with a sign: *Jesus has just left the building*.

He thought about the movie he had finished watching by now.

He asked himself if the sexual protagonist's frustration was the root cause of his ideological fanaticism.

He asked himself about the meaning of the sign: *Jesus has just left the building*.

Perhaps that too conveyed something.

Night was falling, and the time for going out was approaching.

Sklonio je raspeće u fioku i počeo da se sprema.

Proleće je najavljivalo vulgarno razgolićene žene, ofanzivu muškog šarma, povećano trošenje novca.

Sve sama iskušenja kojima treba odoleti.

U džep od jakne stavio je široku lepljivu traku.

Zalepiće je sebi na usta ukoliko se raznaeži pred nekim od tih izazova.

He put away the crucifixion into a drawer, and began to get ready.

The coming spring promised scantily dressed women, male charm on the offensive, increased spending.

All of these sins he would have to resist.

He stuffed a thick roll of masking tape into his jacket pocket.

He would just have to strap it over her mouth if he were to weaken in the face of these temptations.

## Preobražaj

Uhvaćen u mrežu nedeljnih porodičnih ručkova, uspavan tapšanjem po ramenima od svojih bližnjih, živeo je povučeno, bez ambicija.

Nije mogao da bude naivniji.

Statirao je u sopstvenom životu i našao se potpuno zatečen udarcima dobijenim kada je promolio glavu u javnost.

Iznenadio je sam sebe željom da se suprotstavi.

Pun jarosti, smišljao je osvetu neprijateljima koji su vrebali iza sjajnih fasada nedeljnika, obitavali u gnjecavom sivilu dnevnih novina, krili se u virtuelnom gustišu internet stranica.

U sebi je otkrio predele brutalnosti, tajna postrojenja za proizvodnju mraka koja su radila čak i dok je spavao.

Otkriće tog opasnog, izvitoperenog sveta dalo mu je beskrajno samopouzdanje u uspinjanju na društvenoj lestvici.

Ljudi su počeli da ziru od njega, uvažavaju njegove novootkrivene moći.

Jedino njegova žena nije mogla da se pomiri s tim kako on nije više onaj za kojeg se udala.

I dalje je od njega očekivala „ljubav" i „razumevanje", čemu se on smejao kao ženskoj površnosti.

Zaposlio se u industriji prerade zagađenog vazduha u sveže snove i nije imao vremena za gubljenje.

# Metamorphosis

Caught in a web of Sunday family lunches, drowsy from leaning into the shoulders of those close to him, he settled into a reclusive life, without any ambition.

He couldn't be more naïve.

He'd become an extra in the movie of his own life and found himself completely caught off guard by the blows received when occasionally he ventured out into public.

Still, he surprised himself with his desire to fight back.

Filled with hatred, he began to devise vengeance against his enemies who preyed upon him from behind the glossy covers of the weeklies, living in the doughy greyness of daily newspint, hiding within the virtual thicket of internet pages.

Within himself he found regions filled with brutality, secret factories for the production of darkness which kept working even while he slept.

Discovering that lethal, perverted world inflated his self-confidence, with no limits for climbing the social ladder.

People began to back off from him, out of fear for his newly acquired powers.

Only his wife could not reconcile the fact that he was no longer the one she had married.

She still expected "love" and "understanding" from him, a notion he scoffed at as a feminine weakness.

Soon he landed a job in the business of transforming polluted air into fresh dreams. He had no time to lose.

## Avioni budućnosti

...Čvrsto je stezao veslo i oprezno, skoro sa strahopoštovanjem, zasecao tamnu površinu reči, rečenica, tačaka, zareza, ravnomerno, levo-desno, levo-desno.

Neprijatelj je vrebao duž obale, patrolirao naoružan sumanutom tehnologijom: mobilnim telefonima, internetom, spravama za čitanje elektronskih knjiga.

Sa svetim spisima na srcu, s drvenom kašikom i činijom u pastirskoj torbici, nadao se da će mu umaći.

Prošao je tešku deonicu na kojoj su ga brzaci rečenica bacali na oštre stene eksperimentalne proze, nosili ka opasnim virovima novih književnih teorija.

Nekako se domogao mirnog toka.

Trenutak predaha dobro će mu doći, ali zloslutni zvuk koji se čuo postajao je sve jači.

Video je avione kako jedan za drugim uzleću i odlaze.

I ostavljaju ga samog....

Probudio se u znoju.

Neprestano je sanjao jedan te isti san – kako ga svi napuštaju.

Ustao je umoran, obrijao se, obukao odelo i krenuo na posao.

Bezvoljno se peo mermernim stepeništem obrazovne institucije u kojoj je radio.

Čekao ga je naporan dan:

Plovidba plićacima linearnog pripovedanja.

Komandovanje porcelanskim vrapcima-boemima s dugim

## Airplanes of the Future

...He kept a tight grip on the oars and carefully, almost ritually, cut into the surfaces of words, sentences, periods, commas, balancing left-right, left-right.

Along the coastline, lurked his enemy, armed with mad technology for their partrol: cell phones, internet, devices for reading electronic books.

With sacred texts pressed to his heart, and nothing but a wooden spoon and bowl in his shepherd's bag, he hoped he would escape them.

He passed through a tricky sluice where rapids of words tossed him onto the sharp rocks of experimental prose, whishing him towards the perilous torrents of new literary theory.

Somehow he reached a calm pool.

A moment of rest would serve him well, but an ominous sound he heard was becoming even louder.

He noticed how on the horizon, one by one, airplanes took off and departed.

And they left him alone...

He woke up in a cold sweat.

Still, he kept having this same recurring dream—how everyone was abandoning him.

He woke up tired, so he shaved, put on a suit, and went to work.

Miserable, he climbed the marble stairs of the college where he worked.

An exhausting day lay ahead of him:

Sailing in the shallow waters of linear narration.

Dictating to porcelain barnyard swallows and long-bearded

bradama.

Izvođenje zahtevnih gimnastičkih figura u tesnim i slabo osvetljenim ulicama književne tradicije.

Stegnuo je zube i krenuo na čas.

Zavrnuo je rukave i još marljivije nego ranije nastavio da savija mlado drveće samo na jednu stranu.

bohemians.

Performing complex gymnastic routines in the claustrophobic, dimly lit streets of literary tradition.

He clenched his teeth, and he headed off to class.

He rolled up his sleeves and, more diligently than ever, continued to bend the young trees on one side only.

## Napušten od svetova

Prišao je ogledalu i dugo zurio u opuštene kesice ispod očiju.

Taj umorni spoljašnji krajolik učinio mu se jednako tužan kao i unutrašnji.

Dok se okrenuo, čitav jedan svet je nestao iz njegovog života.

„Planeta će ostati biljkama. Ljudi su predodređeni za nebesa", prisetio se reči jednog francuskog pisca.

Bezuspešno je pokušavao da u reči „nebesa" pronađe bar delić nekog višeg, utešnijeg značenja, kad se obreo u vozu.

Kompozicija je bila sablasno prazna, hladna i slabo osvetljena.

Bio je jedini putnik u njoj.

Zaustavio se u vagon-restoranu.

Glas iz zvučnika monotono je ponavljao:

„Ne učestvuj na aukciji književnosti, tom karnevalu ogledala...

...Izgradi svoj tržni centar, zastakli svoj Vavilon...

...Spali sve deponije izgovora...

...Ne učestvuj na aukciji književnosti, tom karnevalu ogledala... Zastakli svoj Vavilon... "

Trgnuo se kad je ponovo začuo: „Spali sve deponije izgovora... "

Još uvek je stajao pred ogledalom i zurio u svoje iznureno lice.

Duboko je uzdahnuo i izašao na terasu.

Soliteri u daljini ličili su na krstarice usidrene u mraku.

Zažmurio je.

Kada je ponovo otvorio oči, prostor ispred njega bio je skoro pust.

## Abandoned by Worlds

He approached a mirror and stared a long time at the bags under his eyes.

The depleted outside world seemed to him equally as sad as the inside one.

But, as he turned, the entire realm disappeared from his life.

"The planet will be left to the plants. People are destined for the heavens," he recalled one French writer saying.

Without success, he sought traces of a more comforting sense of the word "heavens" until he found himself on a train.

Cold and poorly lit, the passenger cars were eerily empty.

He was the only passenger.

He stopped at the café car.

A monotone voice from the speaker kept repeating:

"Do not take part in the sale of literature, that carnival of mirrors…

Build your own shopping mall, glass in your own Babylon…"

Burn all landfills of pronunciation.

Do not participate in the auctioning of literature, that carnival of mirrors…Glass in your Babylon…

He stirred when he heard again: "Burn all landfills of pronunciation…"

Still standing in front of the mirror and staring into his haggard face, he took a deep breath and went out onto the terrace.

Skyscrapers in the distance anchored themselves like cruise ships in darkness.

He closed his eyes.

When he opened them again, the space before him was almost empty.

Soliteri su bezglasno nestajali u noći.
Začuđeno je gledao kako ga i spoljašnji svet napušta.
Mesec se smeškao, bez namere da preduzme nešto.

The skyscrapers were fading into the night without a sound.

Surprised he saw how even the outside world was abandoning him.

With no intention of intervening, the moon simply smiled.

## O mladosti i stvarima koje bi trebalo da su istinite

Koračao je s velikom uramljenom fotografijom u rukama.
(Crni flor bio je prebačen preko gornjeg desnog ugla rama.)
Trideset godina je prošlo, a on je još uvek nosio fotografiju te mrtve devojke.
Njen ubica još uvek je neumorno radio visoko zamahujući tupim, okrvavljenim sečivom.

(Dok je svet podrhtavao
i Venera broj 17 odlazila s punim koferima
i čedni muškarci izvršavali sepuku
i major Tom gubio kontrolu.)

Koračao je, dok se ogromna praznina širila u njemu.
Nije nameravao da istupi iz povorke.

## About Youth and Things That Should Be Truthful

In his hands he carried a photo in a large frame.
(A black ribbon was draped across the upper right corner of the frame.)
Though thirty years had passed, he still held onto the photo of that dead girl.
Still, her killer was working, tirelessly swinging that blunt, bloodied blade.

(All the while the world kept trembling
with Venus number 17 departing with stuffed suitcases
with chaste men committing *seppuku*
with Major Tom losing control.)

He walked, while empty space widened inside him.
He had no intention of leaving the procession.

## Izlet

Bio je skloniji maštanju nego radu, opravdanjima nego borbi.

Sanjareći, stvarao je svetove, ali to mu nije pomagalo da se otrgne osećaju promašenosti.

Činilo mu se da je neko odozgo, iz svemira, spustio crevo iz koga neprestano izlazi uspavljujući gas.

U tome je nalazio razlog za gotovo sve svoje nevolje.

Često je bio prinuđen da hoda u oblaku suvog leda.

Nikako nije mogao da ga se otrese.

Poput slepca, morao je da vodi dresiranog vučjaka kako bi mu pomogao u prelasku ulice.

Jednog dana vučjak mu je rekao:

„Ako nemaš život, stvori ga."

To kao da ga je probudilo.

Gurnuo je ruku u sećanja i izvukao jedan od svetova stvorenih sanjarenjem.

Ušao je u njega i spremno prihvatio pravila koja su tamo vladala.

Kupio je crnu pelerinu i jezovitu gumenu masku, krezubog odvratnog starca.

S maskom na licu i kapuljačom preko glave, u dva-tri posle ponoći, uvlačio se u dvorišta jednospratnih ili montažnih kuća gde su živele starice.

Kucao je u prozorska okna, noktima grebao po metalnim simsovima, pesnicom lupao u tanke zidove.

Čekao bi da neka od prepadnutih jadnica proviri iza zavese, a potom bi prstom pokazao na nju i žurno nestajao u noći.

Rezultati su došli brzo.

Jedna od starica koje je uplašio umrla je pokošena infarktom

# Picnic

He was more attuned to fantasy than to work, more to excuses than to conflict.

His daydreams created whole worlds, but that did not help him overcome his sense of failure.

It seemed to him someone from above, from outer space, had lowered a hose from which seeped gas.

In that he found the cause for almost all his problems.

Too often he was forced to walk on a cloud of dry ice.

And he just couldn't shake it off.

As if a blind man, he had to hitch himself to a trained German shepherd, so it could help him cross the street.

Then one day the German shepherd said to him,

"If you don't have a life, create one!"

That seemed to awaken him.

He shoved his arm into memories and drew out one of the worlds from his daydreams.

He stepped into it and immediately accepted the laws that governed there.

He bought a black cape and the vile rubber mask of a toothless, ugly, old man.

With the mask on his face and the hood over his head, from two to three a.m., he would sneak into the yards of one-story prefabs where old ladies usually lived.

He tapped on their window panes, scratched with his nails their metal sills, then banged on their thin walls with his fist.

He waited for one of the poor, frightened things to peek through the curtain, then wag his finger at her, before hastily disappearing into the night.

The results came about quickly.

One of the old ladies died, struck down from a heart attack

izazvanim prevelikim šokom.

Saznao je to u frizerskom salonu, slučajno, iz članka u lokalnim novinama.

Od tada je počeo redovno da kupuje štampu i s najvećom pažnjom prati crnu hroniku i čitulje.

Rezultat mu je bio važan.

Želeo je da ga dobro zapamte pre nego što se vrati u svoj stari i dosadni život.

caused by the severe shock.

He learned of this, accidentally, from an article in the local newspaper he read at a hair salon.

From then on he began to buy the newspapers regularly to follow the dark chronicles and obituaries with great curiosity.

The results mattered to him!

He wanted to be well noticed before he returned to his old humdrum life.

## Dok su se zveri prikradale

Priključen na aparate, mesecima je ležao bez vidljivih znakova života.

Vraćao se iz neke velike, neobjašnjive daljine.

Želeo je da uputi neki znak sestrama koje su ga obilazile, stavi im do znanja da je živ.

Pokušavao je da pomeri prste, usne, ali uzalud.

Bio je slab i za najmanji pokret.

Ležao je sklopljenih očiju i u mislima pratio grupicu ljudi u kožnim motociklističkim jaknama.

Naročitu pažnju mu je privukla devojka s muškom frizurom i blistavom crnom kacigom pod miškom.

Učinilo mu se da je poznaje, da je dobro poznaje.

Ukazala mu se naga na širokom krevetu, u stanu koji mu je, takođe, odnekud bio poznat.

Poznavao je nameštaj, garderober, veliko ogledalo u sobi.

Iznenada, spazio je senku kako se duž zidova primiče devojci.

Visoki muškarac širokih ramena prilazio je njenoj postelji.

Želeo je da krikne i devojku upozori na uljeza, ali glava neznanca već se spustila među njene raširene butine.

Čvrsto ga je držala za kosu.

Iznutra ga je nešto snažno pogodilo u grudnu kost.

Naglo je otvorio oči.

Pet meseci, dvadeset dva dana, jedanaest minuta i tri sekunde posle motociklističke nesreće, prvi put je ugledao nebo.

Bilo je sivo.

## While the Beasts Crept in

Connected to life-support tubes, he lay for months with no clear signs of life.

He was returning from some remote, inexplicable place.

He wanted to send a sign to the nurses taking care of him, to let them know he was alive.

He tried moving his fingers, his lips, but in vain.

He was too weak even to make the smallest gesture.

Lying with eyes closed, in his mind he followed a gang in leather motorcycle jackets.

He was especially drawn to a woman with a butch haircut and a bright, black helmet under her arm.

He thought she seemed familiar to him, that he knew her well.

She lay nude on a big bed in his apartment which also, for some reason, seemed familiar to him.

He knew the furniture, the armoire, the huge mirror in that room.

Suddenly, he spotted a shadow along the walls creeping up to the girl.

A tall man with broad shoulders was approaching the bed.

He wanted to scream, to warn the girl of the intruder, but the stranger's head had already lowered itself between her spread legs.

She grasped him tightly by his hair.

Inside something slapped him hard against his chest.

Suddenly he opened his eyes.

Five months twenty-two days eleven minutes and three seconds after the motorcycle accident, he saw the sky for the very first time.

It was grey.

## O otkriću dva izumrla sveta

Imao je potrebu da govori o važnim stvarima, ali predugo ćuteći kao da je izgubio reči.

Malo s kim je i razgovarao.

Dane je provodio čitajući, i tek uveče, kada bi osetio zamor od buljenja u papir, zauzeo bi mesto pred televizorom.

Jedne noći gledao je emisiju o muzičkom pokretu kome je i sam pripadao u mladosti.

Na ekranu su se smenjivali koncertni snimci, spotovi, fotografije muzičara, omoti ploča, naslovne strane novina – svi oni artefakti pokreta koga je nekada smatrao čistim bogojavljenjem.

Iznenadila ga je spoznaja da ništa u njemu nije zatreperilo, zatitralo.

Ugasio je televizor, ne odgledavši kraj emisije.

Izašao je na terasu da popuši cigaretu.

Dočekao ga je topao, lepljiv vazduh.

Jara koja nije popuštala danima ostavila je požutelo lišće na drveću, spržene travnjake, beživotne ulice.

Gledao je u pustoš pred sobom i razmišljao o onome šta mu se dogodilo.

„Ja sam u stvari mrtav!" spontano je izustio.

Učinilo mu se da je rekao nešto veoma važno.

Nagnuo se preko ograde terase i iz sve snage počeo da viče: „Ja sam mrtav! Mrtav! Čujete li me, ja sam mrtav!"

U mirnoj, skoro nepomičnoj noći, njegov glas je odjekivao po kvartu.

Očekivao je da ljudi izađu na prozore i terase, ali svetla u okolnim stanovima gasila su se jedno za drugim.

## Upon Discovering Two Lost Worlds

He needed to speak about important things but remained silent so long it was as if he couldn't find the words.

He spoke to few people, and then only occasionally.

He spent his days reading, and only in the evening, after he grew tired of staring at newsprint, would he find a spot by the TV.

One night he watched a musical production about a movement he had belonged to in his youth.

Concert recordings, music videos, photographs of musicians, LP covers, front pages of newspapers—kept flashing on the screen—all artifacts of movements he had once considered the world's epiphany.

He was surprised nothing in him fluttered, trembled.

He turned off the TV, before it ended.

He stepped out onto the terrace for a smoke.

He was met by warm, sticky air.

The sweltering heat had not let up for days, leaving yellowed leaves on the trees, lawns burnt, streets lifeless.

He surveyed the devastation before him and considered what had happened.

"I'm actually dead," he said aloud, suddenly.

It seemed he had pronounced something momentous.

He leaned over the railing of the terrace and began shouting at the top of his lungs.

"I am dead! Dead! Can you hear me? Dead!"

In the quiet, almost motionless night, his voice echoed around the quarter.

He expected people would come to their windows and out on their terraces, but the lights in nearby apartments simply went dark, one by one.

## Podignute zavese

Kratke pesme Roberta Bolanja, *Snovi*, kao da su podigle nekakve zavese u njegovoj glavi, pa je i sam počeo da sanja:

Stoji na bini u malom pozorištu, bez publike.
Marsel Prust na svakih pet minuta donosi bukete belih ruža i stavlja ih pred njega.
Oskar Vajld u odeći batlera bez reči uzima te bukete i odnosi ih negde van vidokruga (na deponiju?).
Prust i Vajld, ruku pod ruku, odlaze s bine.
On, nag, na improvizovanom postolju, ostaje s belim kučencetom u rukama koga su mu ostavili na čuvanje.

Radi kao filmski agent i zastupa Franca Kafku.
Odlazi do Dejvida Linča (koji za svoj film o Francu Kafki planira Franca Kafku u glavnoj ulozi) i postavlja mu ultimatum:
„Franc Kafka će glumiti Franca Kafku jedino pod uslovom da se odrekne honorara."
Dejvid Linč na to energično odmahuje rukom.

U odeći Snežane nalazi se na travnatom proplanku.
Umesto patuljaka, oko njega stoji sedam mladih nemačkih pesnika: Brinkman, Fauser, Born, Teobaldi, Delijus, Handke i Vondraček.
Pruža ruke k njima (kao ka deci) i kaže:
„Nažalost, svi ćete biti mrtvi pre nego što postanete

## Lifted Curtains

Somehow, the short poems by Roberto Bolaño, *Dreams*, had raised curtains in his head, so he himself had begun to have dreams:

He is standing on the stage of a small theater, without an audience.
Every five minutes, Marcel Proust brings bouquets of white roses and places them in front of him.
Oscar Wilde, dressed as a butler, without a word, takes these bouquets and carries them out of sight (to the landfill?).
Then hand in hand, Proust and Wilde, exit the stage.
Naked himself, on an improvised pedestal, he stays behind with a white puppy, which they have left in his care.

He works as a movie agent representing Franz Kafka.
He goes to see David Lynch (who for his film about Kafka is planning to cast Franz himself in the lead) and he presents him with an ultimatum.
"Franz Kafka will play Franz Kafka only if he foregoes his fee."

David Lynch enthusiastically waves his hand in agreement.
Wearing the costume of Snow White, he finds himself in a grassy meadow.
Instead of dwarfs, surrounding him stand seven young German poets: Brinkmann, Fauser, Born, Theobaldi, Delius, Handke, and Wondratschek.
He stretches his hands towards them (as if to children), and says,
"Unfortunately, you'll all be dead before you become

slavni.

Osim tebe, Vondraček, ti nećeš biti slavan ni kada umreš."

Potom je prestao da sanja ili se nije sećao svojih snova.
Prvi naredni san koji je zapamtio izgledao je ovako:

Penje se pokretnim stepenicama u aerodromskoj zgradi.
Neka žena kasni na avion.
U žurbi, uspaničena, u želji da ga pretekne, grubo ga odgurne da joj se skloni s puta.
On gubi ravnotežu, pada na leđa i glavom udara o metalnu ivicu stepenika.
Budi se u bolnici i prvo što pita jeste:
„Ko sam ja?"

famous.

That is, except you, Wondratscheck.

You'll never be famous, even after you die."

After that, he stopped dreaming or couldn't remember his dreams.

The next dream he could recall went something like this:

He's riding the escalator up in an airport somewhere.

A woman nearby is late for a plane.

In a hurry, panicked, rushing to pass him, she shoves him rudely from her path.

He loses his balance, falls backwards and bangs his head on the metal edge of a step.

The next thing he knows, he wakes up in a hospital and asks:

"Who am I?"

## U bespućima poezije

Bio je to čudan san.
Iako nije pamtio svoje snove, ovoga se jasno sećao:

A: Dobar dan.
B: Dobar dan.
A: Izvinite, imate li možda zalaske sunca na šumskoj stazi?
B: Pokušajte sutra, možda dobijemo neku količinu.
A: A kapi rose na tek probuđenoj travi?
B: Nemamo.
A: Proplamsaje umirućeg dana?
B: Nemamo ni to.
A: Pa vi ništa nemate!?
B: Izvinite, odakle vam ovaj broj?
A: Od Aligijerija. Lično mi ga je izdiktirao.
B: A tako... Možda bismo ipak mogli da vam pomognemo.
A: Dajte mi nekog od liričara.
B: Odeljenje lirske poezije je na kolektivnom izletu u prirodi, tačnije u voćnjaku.
A: Da, da... Logično, zar ne?... Izvinite, a koga sam dobio?
B: Mrtvačnicu.
A: Pa upravo vas i tražim!
B: Rekli ste da tražite liričare.
A: Ne, pogrešio sam. Tražim ekspresioniste.
B: Jeste li sigurni?
A: Potpuno siguran... Izvinite, a s kim razgovaram?
B: Doktor Ben kraj telefona. Ben, Gotfrid Ben. A vi ste?

## In the Wilderness of Poetry

It was an unusual dream.

Even though he never remembers his dreams, he remembered this one clearly:

A: Good day.

B: Good day.

A: Excuse me, do you perhaps have sunsets on the forest trail?

B: Try tomorrow, we might get some.

A: And a dew on a just awoken grass?

B: We don't have it.

A: Flares of a dying day?

B: We don't have those either.

A: So, you don't have anything!?

B: Sorry, where did you get this number?

A: From Alighieri. He dictated it to me personally.

B: Oh, I see... Perhaps we can help you after all.

A: Please, give me one of the lyricists.

B: The whole lyrical poetry department is on a picnic in the woods, to be exact, in an orchard.

A: Yes, of course...Logical, isn't it?... Excuse me, and to whom am I speaking?

B: The morgue.

A: Well, you're exactly the one I was trying to reach!

B: You said you wanted the lyricists.

A: No, I made a mistake. I am looking for the expressionists.

B: Are you sure?

A: Absolutely sure... Sorry, to whom am I speaking?

B: Dr. Benn on the phone. Benn, Gottfried Benn. And you are?

A: Kampuš, Alvaro de Kampuš.

B: Gospodine Kampuš, koliko je meni poznato, vama je potrebna trafika, a ne mrtvačnica.

A: Na trafiku upravo gledam, potrebna mi je mrtvačnica.

B: Ipak je greška. Ovde odeljenje lirskih pesnika.

A: Ali rekli ste da je mrtvačnica.

B: Izvinite, pogrešio sam.

A: Onda, doviđenja. Javiću se sutra ponovo, povodom onih zalazaka sunca.

B: Doviđenja. Slobodno pozovite...

Pitao se otkud mu takav san.

On uopšte nije voleo poeziju, ponajmanje lirsku.

Ni za imena koja se pominju u snu nikada nije čuo.

Ličila su mu na imena fudbalera, naročito taj Alvaro de Kampuš.

Mogao se zakleti da je to neki portugalski internacionalac.

A i taj Aligijeri... on bi mogao biti Argentinac, eventualno Italijan, neki vezni, klupski igrač.

Jedino mu ime tog Bena, Gotfrida Bena nije delovalo da ima veze s fudbalom.

Uostalom, predstavio se kao doktor.

Ipak, zamislio ga je kao vlasnika fudbalskog kluba sklonog nedoličnom ponašanju, kako, s čašom viskija u desnoj i tompusom u levoj ruci, poslovnim partnerima recituje gadosti u uho.

Zamislio je potom i sebe, kako izbačen s nekakvog tobogana leti visoko, probija negostoljubivu izmaglicu tog sna i pada na

A: Campos, Alvaro de Campos.

B: Mr. Campos, as far as I know, you need the tobacco shop, not the morgue.

A: I'm looking at a tobacco shop. I need the morgue.

B: Even so, this is a mistake. This is the lyrical poetry department.

A: But you said it was the morgue.

B: Sorry, I made a mistake.

A: Then, goodbye. I'll be back again tomorrow, with regards to those sunsets.

B: Goodbye. Please feel free to call.

He wondered where that kind of dream could have come from.

He didn't like poetry at all, least of all lyrical poems.

He had never even heard of the names that were mentioned in the dream.

They resembled names of soccer players, especially Alvaro de Campos.

He could swear that he was one of the Portuguese internationals.

And that Alighieri... he could be Argentinian or perhaps Italian, some midfielder, club player.

Only the name of that Benn, Gotfried Benn, didn't seem as if it had anything to do with soccer.

Anyhow, he introduced himself as a doctor.

Still, he imagined him as the owner of a soccer club prone to inappropriate behavior, who with a glass of whiskey in his right hand, and a cigar in his left, recites abominations into his business partners' ears.

He then imagined himself, having been thrown off some kind of a toboggan flying high, cutting inhospitable mist of that

ogromnu srebrnu jelku grana otežalih od snega.

    Tu je već bio na svom terenu, što mu je predstavljalo veliko olakšanje.

dream and falling onto a huge silver fir tree heavy with snow.

There he was already in his own territory, which represented a great relief.

## Popodne jednog Fauna

Čim je otpratio ženu kod majke, spremio se i pošao u nabavku pića.

Imao je vikend pred sobom.

Dobro raspoloženje počeo je da mu kvari sused na izlazu iz zgrade.

Dok su razgovarali, komšija ga je sve vreme tapšao po ramenu.

Gledao ga je pravo u oči i poltronski klimao glavom na svaku njegovu reč.

Da li mu je time stavljao do znanja „da zna"?

Frizerka, kod koje je tog popodneva imao zakazano šišanje, raspričala se bez ikakvog povoda o svojoj novoj pripravnici.

„Seksi lutkica", opisala je frizerka sedamnaestogodišnju učenicu srednje frizerske koja je pohađala praksu u njenom salonu.

To nije moglo biti slučajno.

Zašto bi baš njemu pričala o nekoj seksi-tinedžerki, devojci od koje je skoro trostruko stariji?

U povratku je sreo studenta književnosti, komšiju s drugog sprata.

Dok su čekali lift student ga je pozvao kod sebe na žurku, govoreći kako će doći i neke brucoškinje koje su kao „puštene s lanca".

To mu se učinilo kao nova provokacija.

Šta su svi oni želeli da mu kažu?

Da li nešto znaju ili samo slute?

Došao je kući, istuširao se i obrijao.

Spremao se da sipa sebi piće, kada mu je zazvonio mobilni telefon.

# Afternoon of a Faun

As soon as he saw his wife off to her mother's, he got dressed and went out to get drinks.

He had a weekend ahead of him.

His good mood began to change when he met his neighbour at the exit of the building.

While they were talking, the neighbour tapped his shoulder the whole time.

He looked him straight in the eye and, obediently, nodded his head at each one of his words.

Was he trying to let him know that he "knows?"

The hairdresser, at whose salon he had an appointment that afternoon, started talking without any reason about her new trainee.

"Sexy doll," the hairdresser described the seventeen-year old hairdressing high school student who was doing her internship at the salon.

That couldn't have been accidental.

Why would she be telling him specifically about some sexy teenager, a girl he was nearly three times older than.

On the way back he met a literature student, his second floor neighbor.

While they waited for the elevator, the student asked him over to his place for a party, saying how some "off the chain," freshman girls would also be coming.

That seemed to him like a new provocation.

What were they all trying to tell him?

Do they know something or do they only suspect?

He arrived home, showered and shaved.

He was about to pour himself a drink, when his cell phone rang.

Broj je bio skriven.
Nasmešio se i pritisnuo zeleno dugme.
„Da", rekao je raspoložen.

The number was withheld.
He smiled and pressed the green button.
"Yes," he said, feeling good now.

## Slučaj službenika reklamne agencije

„Razmišljaj! Oslobodi reči! Oslobodi misli!", urlao je na sebe u svojoj radnoj sobi.

Radio je kao kopirajter u marketinškoj agenciji, s privilegijom da posao obavlja od kuće.

Obično se budio oko dva popodne i najpre bi s nogu drmnuo nešto žestoko.

Tako se najbolje rasanjivao.

Redosled je potom bio ustaljen: kafa, rakija, pivo, ponekad i vino, u zavisnosti šta je imao u kućnom baru.

Uveče bi, za podizanje kreativnosti, popušio džoint-dva.

Bili su mu neophodni stimulansi dok je tražio adekvatne reči (proleće, mladost, optimizam...) koje bi bespućima banalnosti pomogle da izgledaju manje jeftino, ili bar prihvatljivo običnom potrošaču.

Ni sam nije znao kako ga do sada nisu otpustili.

Za pola godine provedene u firmi, od dvadesetak ideja koje je smislio i predložio, samo dve su postale reklame.

Jedna od njih bila je postavljena u ulici u kojoj je živeo i mogla se videti s njegove terase.

Na bilbordu je poznata estradna zvezda reklamirala čaj za mršavljenje, dok su joj se ogromne silikonske grudi prelivale iz dubokog dekoltea i pretile da padnu na prolaznike.

Nije se ponosio svojim radom.

Čitav posao s reklamama bio je daleko od njegovih pravih interesovanja.

Bar je tako voleo da misli o sebi – kako još uvek ima nekakva „prava" interesovanja.

## The Case of an Advertising Agency Employee

"Think! Free the words! Free your mind!" he was shouting at himself in his home office.

He worked as a copy writer in a marketing agency, with the privilege of being able to work from home.

Usually he woke up at two p.m. and he would first take a swig of something strong.

That was the best way for him to wake up.

The schedule after that was routine: coffee, brandy, beer, sometimes wine, depending on what he had available in his home bar.

In the evening, in order to increase his creativity, he would smoke a joint or two.

Stimuli were necessary to him while he searched for the adequate words (spring, youth, optimism…) which would help the wasteland of banality to appear less cheap, or at least to appeal to the average consumer.

He, himself, had no idea why he hadn't been fired yet.

For the half year he had spent in the company, from the twenty or so ideas that he had come up with and proposed, only two were turned into ads.

One of these was placed on the street where he lived and could be seen from his balcony.

On the billboard a famous female star singer was advertising a weight loss tea, while her huge silicone breasts were bursting out of their cleavage and threatened to fall onto passersby.

He was not proud of his work.

The whole job with ads was far away from his "true" interests.

At least that was how he liked to think of himself—that he still had some kind of "real" interest.

U mladosti je pisao poeziju.

Zbirka pesama koju je tada objavio sve više su mu se činila kao nešto što ga može opravdati.

Promukao od urlanja, sedeo je za radnim stolom i zurio u pepeljaru punu opušaka.

I pored uobičajenih podsticaja ideje nikako nisu dolazile.

Ispio je pivo i izašao na terasu.

Praznu limenku hitnuo je na travnjak ispred zgrade, tiho opsovao i vratio se u sobu da nastavi s radom.

Dole na trotoarima ljudi su hodali zagledani u vrhove svojih cipela, u ekrane svojih mobilnih telefona.

Psi su dremali u haustorima.

Daleko u blokovima nazirala se svetlost, obrisi života.

In his youth he had written poetry.

The poetry collection he published then seemed to him like something that could validate him.

His voice cracking from screaming, he was sitting at his desk and staring at the ashtray filled with cigarette butts.

In spite of the usual incentives, ideas weren't coming to him.

He drank a beer and then went out onto the balcony.

He threw the empty can onto the lawn in front of the building, quietly swore, and then he softly returned to the room to continue with the work.

Below on the sidewalks, people walked, staring at the tips of their shoes, into the screens of their cell phones.

Dogs were sleeping in the hallways.

Far in the apartment blocks there was a glimpse of light, contours of life.

## Književnost i nasilje

Prekraćivao je samoću beleženjem misli.
*Ja sam komad nameštaja koji brže od ostalih delova prikuplja prašinu* – zapisao je u dnevniku.
Nije znao otkud mu to, ali verovao je u istinitost automatskog pisanja, pa rečenicu nije precrtao.
Sedeo je zamišljen i gledao kroz prozor.
Razmišljao je o čileanskom pesniku opsednutim književnošću i nasiljem.
Pitao se da li je potreban talenat kako bi neko postao kriminalac.
Odložio je papir i olovku i pošao po čašu vode.
Prolazeći pored ogledala u hodniku spazio je sebe i vrisnuo od užasa.
Patuljasti duh čovekoljublja na njegovom ramenu imao je crnu fantomku na glavi.

## Literature and Violence

He was diminishing loneliness by writing down his thoughts.

*I'm the piece of furniture which collects dust faster than other parts*, he wrote in his journal.

He had no idea where that came from, but he believed in the authenticity of automatic writing, so he didn't erase the sentence.

He sat deep in thoughts and looked out of the window.

He was thinking of the Chilean poet obsessed with literature and violence.

He asked himself if one needed talent to become a criminal.

He sat his paper and pencil aside and went to get a glass of water.

Passing by the mirror in the hallway, he saw himself and shrieked from horror.

The dwarf-like ghost of philanthropy sitting on his shoulder wore a black ski mask over his head.

## Sirotica

Privlačili su ga čudaci, fascinirale samoubice, divio se ukletim pesnicima.

Upoznavao se sa svakim depresivcem i ego-manijakom kojeg bi sreo (s nekima od njih je čak i sklapao prijateljstva), ali sve to nije značilo da i sam ima dijagnozu.

Ipak, predstavljao se kao podvojena ličnost.

Nije imao nijedan simptom koji bi ukazivao na taj psihički poremećaj, ali uporno je ponavljao kako negde duboko u njemu živi i druga ličnost – Margareta, sirotica zarobljena u mraku.

Njegova prva ličnost žestoko se protivila tome, tvrdeći da njena suparnica ne postoji.

Navodna podvojenost je izmišljotina dokonog uma, želja za privlačenjem pažnje.

Uzalud se opirao prvoj ličnosti pozivanjem na zakon o zaštiti ugroženih grupa i pojedinaca, na pluralizam identiteta – prva ličnost nije odstupala od tvrdnje da je čitava igra osmišljena.

U nemogućnosti da prvoj ličnosti pruži bilo kakav dokaz o postojanju sirotice, osim njenog imena i izgleda (što se nije moglo proveriti), pribegao je manevru lažne predaje.

Odustao je od svojih tvrdnji, uz klauzulu:

*Ukoliko se utvrdi da Margareta ne postoji ili postoji samo kao privid (te se može smatrati lakšom devijacijom psihe), prva ličnost, saznanje da je jedina, ne sme primiti s prevelikim oduševljenjem niti likovanjem.*

# A Waif

He was drawn to weirdos, and fascinated by people who commit suicide, yet he admired cursed poets.

He got to know all kinds of depressed individuals and egomaniacs whom he'd meet (he'd even befriended some of them), but all that didn't mean that he himself had been diagnosed with a mental illness.

Still, he introduced himself as having a split personality.

He had no symptoms which would point to that psychological disorder, but he constantly repeated how deep inside him lived another person—Margareta, a waif captured in darkness.

His first personality was seriously objecting to that, claiming that his female rival didn't exist.

The supposed split was a made up story of an idle mind, a desire to attract attention.

In vain he resisted that first personality, calling upon the law protecting underrepresented groups and individuals, of the pluralism of identity, although that first personality didn't give up on insisting that the whole game was premeditated.

Being unable to give any kind of proof to the first personality that the waif really existed, except for her name and her looks (which couldn't be verified), he resorted to the maneuver of false surrender.

He gave up on his assertions, with a clause:

*If it is determined that Margareta doesn't exist or exists only as an illusion (and can therefore be considered as a mild deviation of the psyche), the first being, upon the acknowledgement of being the only one, cannot show too much enthusiasm or glee.*

Potpisao je te ništavne reči i tako Margaretu oslobodio iz kaveza.

Njeno postojanje zabeleženo je na papiru i overeno pečatom.

Bio je to presudni korak u legalizaciji njenog postojanja.

Preuzimanje vlasti biće manje-više rutinska stvar.

Počeo je s planovima kakve cipele, haljinu i nakit da joj kupi.

Moraće da izgleda kao kraljica dok crvenim tepihom bude hodala do trona.

He signed these worthless words and with this liberated Margareta from the cage.

Her existence was noted on paper and was validated with a seal.

That was the key step to legalizing her existence.

Taking control here would be more or less a routine thing.

He began to plan on what type of shoes, dresses and jewellery to buy for her.

She had to look like a queen as she walked to the throne on the red carpet.

## Borba Titana

Čak i kada je raskrinkao sve njihove laži i otišao od njih, još uvek su ga opterećivali svojim nevidljivim prisustvom.

Sedeli su u mraku i merili svaku njegovu reč, procenjivali svaki njegov postupak, strpljivo čekali na njegov telefonski poziv.

Trudio se da ne razmišlja o njima i ne pridaje važnost njihovim prećutnim očekivanjima, ali znao je da će biti potpuno slobodan tek kada ih sahrani i isplati grobare po obavljenom poslu.

Nije se usuđivao da spali porodične fotografije.

U sitnom rasteru crnobelih senki skrivalo se previše duhova zdravih zuba i mršavih lica, defilovalo previše jeftinih bluza i prekratkih pantalona, smenjivalo se previše naivnog optimizma i prerane ozbiljnosti...

Bilo je previše, previše toga što ih je jačalo.

A oni?

Oni su sedeli u svojim foteljama i mršavim, žilavim rukama čvrsto držali slušalicu telefona u koju su izgovarali naređenja u formi molbe.

Za razliku od njega koji je posedovao svet, oni su posedovali moć.

Ipak, njegovu nepobedivost to uopšte nije zanimalo.

## The Battle of the Titans

Even when he debunked all their lies and moved away from them, they still burdened him with their invisible presence.

They sat in darkness measuring his every word, evaluating his every move, and patiently waiting for his next phone call.

He tried not to think of them, not to give any importance to their tacit expectations, but he knew that he would be completely free only after they were buried and the gravediggers were paid off after completing the job.

He didn't dare burn the family photographs.

Too many ghosts with healthy teeth and gaunt faces were hiding in the small bits of black and white shadows; too many cheap blouses and overly short pants were parading; too much naive optimism and untimely seriousness changed one following the other...

There simply was too much, too much of that which strengthened them.

And what about them?

They were sitting in their armchairs firmly holding receivers in their skinny, sinewy palms as they stated orders in the form of petitions.

In contrast to him who possessed the world, they possessed all the power.

Still, his invincibility wasn't interested in that, not at all.

## Sudar mišljenja u različitim vremenskim zonama

Kao poslednji kandidat za posao, čekao je ispred kancelarije glavnog urednika.

Spremao se da kaže kako su koncept i identitet obavezujuće stvari u 21. veku.

Štampati zbirke poezije danas, pa to je smešno.

Jedina dužnost čoveka je da misli, a ne da „oseća".

Duh vremena moramo zgrabiti za vrat i naterati ga da nam se „ispiša po tepihu".

Pozvali su ga da uđe u trenutku dok je razmišljao o pretencioznosti svoje poslednje misli.

Ipak, odlučio je da baš njome započne razgovor.

Samouverenost je odlika lidera, to će im jasno staviti do znanja.

Svoje viđenje buduće postavke posla nije obrazlagao ni pet minuta, kada ga je glavni urednik prekinuo i zahvalio mu se na dolasku.

Izašao je iz kancelarije gotovo zapanjen.

Nije mogao ni da pretpostavi kako još uvek postoje oni koji poeziju smatraju „najvišim oblikom odgovornosti" (i da čovek zaslužuje raj).

Tu nešto nije bilo u redu.

A onda su mu se misli zaustavile.

## Clash of Opinions in Different Time Zones

As the final job candidate, he waited in front of the office of the editor-in-chief.

He was getting ready to say how concept and identity are the confining issues in the 21st century.

Publishing collections of poetry today? Why, that's a joke!

The only duty of a person is to think, not to "feel."

We must grab the spirit of time by the neck and force it "to pee on the carpet."

They invited him in at the moment when he was thinking about the pretentiousness of his last thought.

Even so, he decided to begin the conversation exactly with that.

Self-confidence is a reflection of a leader, which he will make clear to them.

An explanation of his vision of the future organization of the work lasted not even five minutes, when the editor-in-chief stopped him and thanked him for coming.

He left the office quite stunned.

He could not have even imagined that there still exist those who consider poetry "the highest form of responsibility" (and that a human being deserves heaven).

Something there was not right.

And then his thoughts stopped.

## Hronika najavljenog nestanka

Novac, novac, novac, krčalo je na svakom koraku.
„Čemu toliko truda ako svi završavamo na istom mestu", razmišljao je.
Potrebno je uneti bar malo avanture u život.
Čovek mora nekako da zabavlja sebe.
Pitao se šta da promeni.
Šta da uradi, a da to ne bude nešto obično, svakodnevno.
Nestaće?
Tako je. Nestaće kao Hudini.
Još bolje, nestaće zauvek.
Izgubiće se negde u svetu pod lažnim imenom.
Ta ideja naročito mu se dopala.
Odluka je sazrela brzo.
Biće to najavljeni nestanak.
Počeo je da sastavlja i oproštajni govor.
Okupiće prijatelje i saopštiće im šta namerava.
Neće mu verovati, smejaće se, odmahivaće rukom.
„Svaki veliki podvig isprva se čini kao nemoguć", podsetiće ih.
Oni će se smejati još više i upirati prstom u njega.
„Nikad ne potcenjujte nevinu dušu", dodaće.
Ulepšaće govor još nekom frazom, bar mu reči nikada nisu nedostajale.
„Dame i gospodo, bacimo kocke", tako će početi.

## Chronicle of a Preset Disappearance

Money, money, money, there were murmurs at every step.

"What's the point of so much effort when we all end up in the same place anyway," he thought.

It's necessary to bring at least a little bit of adventure in one's life.

And a man must entertain himself.

He wondered what he could change.

What to do so it wasn't something common, ordinary.

Disappear?

That's it. Like Houdini, he will disappear.

Even better, he will disappear forever.

He'll get lost some place in the world under a false name.

The idea seemed especially appealing to him.

The decision ripened quickly.

It will be an announced disappearance.

He also began to compose his farewell speech.

He'll get together with his friends to let them know his plans.

They won't believe him, they will laugh, waving their hands.

"Each great achievement at first seems impossible," he'll remind them.

They will laugh again even more and point at him.

"Never underestimate an innocent soul," he'll add.

He will embellish the speech with some elaborate phrases since at least he's never short of the right words.

"Ladies and gentlemen, let's throw the dice," that's how it'll begin.

## Dugokose muzičke sirene

U ponoć, stajao je skriven iza stabla platana i posmatrao kolonu aveti kako prolazi ulicom.
Mutno ulično svetlo jedva je razmicalo tamu, ali jasno je video lica tih odavno mrtvih ljudi.
Mnoge od njih je poznavao, s nekima se i družio.
Odevene u kao sneg bele toge, aveti su podizale ruke i ponavljale:
„Mir! Ljubav! Anarhija!", mantre koje je nekada i sam izgovarao.
Te reči načas su ga vratile u prošlost.
Setio se trenutka kada su svi oni, i on s njima, prvi put čuli dozivanja dugokosih muzičkih sirena s električnim gitarama.
Imao je tada petnaest i živeo sam s majkom.
I setio se kako je svakoga dana morao u šumu da nahrani ptice i donese drva, te nije stizao da zajedno s drugovima pohrli u susret tom ljubičastom, i plavom, i modrom dozivanju koje je strujalo ulicama i pločnicima, učionicama i hodnicima, sobama i tavanima.
I učinilo mu se da aveti izgledaju tako lepo, poput rimskih patricija u šetnji, tako nevino, poput dece koja odlaze na izlet, ili se s njega vraćaju.
Zažalio je što nije među njima.
Stajao je leđima oslonjen o stablo platana.
Stiskao je usne da ne zaplače, odlučan da idući put ne ponovi istu grešku.

## Long-Haired Musical Mermaids

At midnight, he stood hidden behind the sycamore tree and watched a column of apparitions passing down the street.

Dim street lighting barely broke through the darkness, but he could clearly see the faces of those long dead people.

Many of them he had known, some were his friends.

Dressed in togas white as snow, the apparitions had their hands raised and were repeating:

"Peace! Love! Anarchy!" mantras which he himself used to utter.

Those words took him back to the past for a moment.

He remembered moments when they all, and he with them, first heard the calling of the long-haired musical mermaids with electric guitars.

He was then fifteen years old and still living with his mother.

And he remembered how each day he had to go to the forest to feed the birds and bring in firewood, so he had no time to rush with his friends to greet the purple, blue, and maroon calling that flowed down streets and pavements, classrooms and hallways, rooms and attics.

And it seemed to him the ghosts looked, like Roman patricians promenading, so nice, so innocent, like children going on a picnic, or returning from one.

He was sorry he was not with them.

He stood with his back leaning against a sycamore tree.

He pressed his lips so as not to cry, determined that the next time he would be sure not to repeat the same mistake.

## Poezija za svačiji dom

Posle mnogo vremena napisao je pesmu.
Zvala se *Oglas* i glasila je:

*Ne voli oružje*
*nije opasan po okolinu*
*nema velike političke ideje*

*ima zdravo srce*
*svakodnevne erekcije*
*očuvan primerak u svakom pogledu*

*prošao krizu tridesetih, četrdesetih*
*sada u pedesetim*
*pred novim odlukama*

*spreman na nekoliko ludih*
*nezaboravnih godina*
*pre nego što se odjavi*

Ona obično nije preturala po njegovim stvarima, ali brišući prašinu, pronašla je pesmu na njegovom radnom stolu.
Kada ju je pročitala, zaljubljeno mu se bacila oko vrata, odlučna da zgrabi i do kraja iskoristi tih njegovih obećanih „nekoliko nezaboravnih" godina pre nego što je napusti.
Za razliku od njega, ona je planirala da živi večno.

## Poetry for Everyone's Home

After a long time he wrote a poem.
It was called "The Ad" and went like this:

*he doesn't like weapons*
*he poses no threat to society*
*he doesn't have big political ideas*

*he has a healthy heart*
*every day erections*
*a preserved copy in every respect*

*he has passed the midlife crisis*
*of his 30s and 40s*
*and now in his 50s has new decisions ahead*

*ready for a few crazy*
*unforgettable years*
*before he checks out*

    She usually didn't go through his things, but while dusting, she found this poem on his desk.
    After she read it, she thrust her arms around his neck lovingly, determined to grab him and use to the very end those promised, "few unforgettable years" before he left her.
    Unlike him, she was planning to live forever.

## Odlučnost srednjih godina

Čitavog života sanjao je okean, autoput duž obale, zrake sunca na niklovanim branicima kabrioleta, ali te slike, sanjive zlatne ribice, ostale su u staklenoj kugli na vitrini njegove nekadašnje momačke sobe.

Kada je napustio roditeljski dom nije ih poneo sa sobom. (Bile su mu preteške za nošenje.)

Svoju prošlost ostavio je svima koji su ga poznavali da je pokradu i iskoriste najbolje delove za svoje autobiografije.

Sebi je namenio budućnost.

Počeo je da vežba jogu, meditira, odlazi na plivanje.

Istrčati maraton – bio je njegov krajnji cilj.

Za to vreme, modna industrija je od odevnih predmeta stvarala poeziju za svačiji garderober.

Za to vreme, žene njegovih drugara u Sent Moricu pile su asam (desetine hiljada indijskih ruku bralo je taj čaj).

Za to vreme, nebo je neumorno menjalo vlasnike i sunce se smeškalo onima što dolaze.

Poput kakvog gordog nacionalnog pesnika, prošlost je blistala nepodnošljivim sjajem, nedodirljiva i samodovoljna.

Nije je primećivao, nije želeo da je primećuje.

## Decisiveness of Middle Age

His whole life he had dreamt of the ocean, the highway by the coast, the sun's rays on the nickel-plated fenders of a convertible, but those images, like sleepy goldfish, remained in their glass bowl on the showcase of his old bachelor's pad.

When he left his parents' home, he did not bring them with him.

(They were too heavy to carry.)

He left his past to everyone who had known him to plunder, making use of the best parts for their own autobiographies.

For himself he set aside the future.

He began to practice yoga, to meditate, to go swimming.

To run a marathon—that was his ultimate goal.

In the meantime, the fashion industry was creating poetry out of clothes, for everyone's closet.

In the meantime, wives of his friends in St. Moritz drank Assam (tens of thousands of Indian hands had picked that tea).

In the meantime, that sky had tirelessly changed owners and the sun shone brightly on those yet to come.

Like some prestigious national poet, the past glistened with an unbearable glimmer, untouchable and self-sufficient.

He did not notice it, he did not wish to notice it.

## Bekstvo nakon kratke molitve

Kod ljudi je najviše mrzeo potrebu za razbacivanjem novca, a ona je preterivala.

Nosila je odeću izrađenu u malim serijama, dizajniranu od strane misterioznih japanskih kreatora.

Kupovala je obuću italijanskih dizajnera za koje nije čuo, koristila parfeme isključivo skandinavskih ekscentrika.

Trošila je na sebe nezamislive količine para.

Često se dešavalo i da ponekom prosjaku udeli nepristojno veliku sumu kao milostinju.

Od samog početka znao je da veza s njom neće potrajati.

Nije bio njena klasa.

Izdržao je mesec dana i shvatio da je vreme za povratak u sopstveni akvarijum.

Mislio je da joj to saopšti obazrivo, biranim rečima, najbolje na nekom javnom mestu.

Želeo je da predupredi njenu burnu reakciju kojima je inače bila sklona.

Izašli su na večeru u restoran koji je ona odabrala.

„Za muškarca je najvažnije da pronađe pravu ženu", počeo je s opštim mestom.

Na krajevima njenih usana zatitrao je osmeh iznad koga su, tako mu se učinilo, u vazduhu razdragano trčkarale srne i skakutali zečevi iz Diznijevih filmova.

Gledala ga je zaljubljeno i čekala da nastavi.

Ti Diznijevi likovi potpuno su ga dekoncentrisali.

## Escape after a Short Prayer

What he hated in people was being frivolous with money, and she overdid it.

She wore clothes made from limited collections created by mysterious Japanese designers.

She bought shoes by Italian designers whose names he had never heard of, used perfumes exclusively by Scandinavian eccentrics.

In short, she spent an unbelievable amount of money on herself.

It often happened that as an act of charity, she would hand an indecently large sum of cash to some beggar.

From the very beginning he knew the relationship with her would not last.

He wasn't in her league.

He stuck it out a month and realised that it was time to return to his own aquarium.

He thought he should break the news carefully, with well-chosen words, best done in a public place.

He wanted to preempt the turbulent reaction to which she was prone.

They went for a dinner at a restaurant that she had picked out.

"The most important thing for a man is to find the right woman," he began at the common ground.

At the edges of her lips, a small quivering smile appeared, above which, he thought he noticed, reindeer happily frolicked in the air, and rabbits jumped out from Disney's movies.

She stared at him lovingly, as she waited for him to continue.

Those Disney characters completely made him lose his concentration.

Našao se zatečen osekom svojih misli, bez ijedne smislene rečenice na vidiku.

Zurio je u tanjir, očajnički se moleći da mu dođe sledeća rečenica.

„Kao i u kockanju, i u ljubavi je najvažniji stav prema gubitku", čuo je kako neko izgovara njegovim glasom.

Pogledao je levo, pa desno; sedeli su sami za stolom u uglu.

Polako je ustao i krenuo u toalet.

Krijući se iza gipsanog stuba i raščupane nolina palme, platio je račun i žurno napustio lokal.

Ona je sedela i čekala ga, ništa ne sluteći.

Okupirana mislima o veličini svojih grudi koje je smatrala premalim, nije obratila pažnju na njegovu poslednju rečenicu.

Znala bi rešenje zagonetke koja ju je opsedala nakon što ga je kroz petnaest minuta pozvala na mobilni telefon, a ljubazan ženski glas joj saopštio da pozvani korisnik trenutno nije dostupan.

He found himself stuck in the low tide of his thoughts, without a single pre-prepared sentence in sight.

He stared at his plate, desperately praying for the next sentence to come to him.

"As in gambling, in love as well, the most important disposition is the one towards loss," he heard someone utter with his voice.

He looked to the left, then to the right; they were sitting alone in a corner.

Slowly he stood up and went to the bathroom.

Hiding behind a plaster cast pillar and the bushy nolina palm, he paid the bill and hastily left the place.

She sat and waited for him without suspecting anything.

Deep in thought about the size of her breasts, which she considered too small, she hadn't paid any attention to his last sentence.

She might have known the answer to the enigma which possessed her, had she called him fifteen minutes later on his cell phone, when a pleasant female voice would tell her that the person in question was unavailable at this time.

## Udarac za udarcem

U rastrzanom polusnu, misli o poeziji povijale su se levo-desno u krošnjama njegovih neurona:
*Pesnici srednje generacije su se istrošili... Novi mehanički prevrću reči... Muze su odbile da rizikuju... Pisanje poezije se pretvara u istraživanje sopstvenog vrta... u izradu domaćeg zadatka iz tradicije...*
Iznenada, teška metalna vrata su se otkačila i s velike visine stropoštala na kuhinjske crno-bele podne pločice, proizvevši jedno monstruozno: Tras!!!
Istog trena se probudio.
Bunovan, pokušao je da se orijentiše u mraku.
Pod zracima uličnog osvetljenja koji su dopirali ispod napola spuštenih roletni prepoznao je komodu, stonu lampu s iscrtanim platnenim abažurom, dvokrilni garderober – nalazio se u svojoj spavaćoj sobi.
Kroz otvorena vrata ušetala je mačka i skočila na krevet.
Potom je na krevet skočio i pas, i čučnuo pored mačke.
On uopšte nije imao ni psa, ni mačku.
A nije imao ni decu.
Užasnut, gledao je u devojčicu kovrdžave plave kose pored kreveta.
Držala je karton s natpisom: *Dobro došao!*
„Samo da nisam u nekom azijskom hororu", promrmljao je.
Nije imao hrabrosti da uključi stonu lampu.

## Blow after Blow

In a distrurbed half-dream state, thoughts of poetry swayed left-right in the treetops of his neurons:

*The poets of the middle generation have burnt out... The new ones mechanically turn over words... The muses have declined to take risks... Writing poetry has turned into an exploration of a personal garden... the mere completion of a homework assignment, in tradition...*

Suddenly, the heavy metal door detached and plunged from great height onto the black and white kitchen floor tiles, producing a monstrous, "Bang!"

Immediately he woke up.

Delirious, he tried to orient himself in the dark.

Under the beams of the street lamps which were reaching through the half-closed blinds, he recognized the dresser, the table lamp with the linen lampshade, the two-door armoire—he was in his bedroom.

A cat walked in through the open door and jumped onto the bed.

Then a dog jumped on the bed and squatted next to the cat.

He did not even own a dog, or a cat.

And he didn't have any children.

Horrified, he looked at a girl with curly, blonde hair standing next to the bed.

She was holding a cardboard sign saying, *Welcome!*

"I hope I'm not in some Asian horror film," he prayed.

He wasn't brave enough to turn on the table lamp.

## Dartovski čovek

Preselio se u drugi, mnogo veći grad, u kome je poznavao samo dva čoveka; jedan od njih bio je izdavač, drugi je bio fotograf.

Fotograf je, pored svog posla, na internetu oformio i vodio zatvorenu grupu od stotinak istomišljenika koji su međusobno razmenjivali mejlove.

Zamolio je fotografa da ga priključi na listu i dao mu svoju imejl adresu.

Od toga dana svakodnevno je dobijao desetak-dvadesetak pisama, uglavnom antiglobalističke sadržine.

Jedno od njih naročito mu je privuklo pažnju:

*Pre otprilike milion godina, došle su kiše i počeo je pleistocen. Loše vreme navelo je čoveka da razvije inteligenciju. Pojavilo se oruđe od oblog kamenja, kao i ručne sekire. Nežni robustus je nestao kada su kiše ustuknule pred periodičnim sušama, ali dartovski čovek, „životinja lošeg vremena", uspeo je da preživi. Budući da je glavna evolucijska prednost dartovskog čoveka bila agresivnost i instinkt za ubijanjem, postepeno je postao dominantna vrsta na zemlji...*

Učinilo mu se da taj imejl nije dobio slučajno.

Bio je nov u gradu, možda mu je neko preko tog pisma poslao važnu poruku.

Pročitao je pismo još jednom i izašao na terasu.

Dugo je gledao u plastične saksije s muškatlama.

## Dartian Man

He moved to a different, much larger city, in which he knew only two men; one of them was a publisher, the other was a photographer.

The photographer, besides doing his job, formed an internet forum of some hundred people who had similar views about which they exchanged emails.

He asked the photographer to include him on the list and gave him his email address.

From that day he received ten to twenty emails daily, mostly regarding anti-globalization.

One of them especially drew his attention:

*Around a million years ago, rains came and the Pleistocene Epoch began. Bad weather forced humans to develop their intelligence. Tools appeared, made of round stone, as well as hand axes. The gentle robustus disappeared as the rain subsided before the perod of droughts, but the Dartian man, "the bad-weather animal," managed to survive. Being that the main evolutionary advantages of the Dartian man were his aggression and his killer instinct, he gradually became the dominant species on Earth...*

It seemed to him that he had not received that email by chance.

He was new to the city, so perhaps someone had sent him an important message through that letter.

He read the email one more time and walked out to the terrace.

He stared at the plastic flowerpots with geraniums for a long time.

Polako im je prišao i bez žurbe, jednu po jednu, polomio sve stabljike.

Vratio se za svoj radni sto pomalo zgrožen sobom, ali zadovoljan.

Prvi test je prošao.

Ako je to mogao da uradi cveću, s ljudima će mu biti mnogo lakše.

He approached them slowly and without hurrying, he broke all their stems, one by one.

He returned to his desk a little disgusted by himself, yet satisfied.

He had passed the first test.

If he could do that to flowers, he could manage much more easily with people.

## Epifanija, mala demonstracija moći

Kako su prolazile godine, postajao je sve rezigniraniji.

Od kako je otišao u penziju, naročito ga je mučilo pitanje boga, misao o prolaznosti, nemogućnost saznanja o onome šta se dešava „posle".

Polako se odvajao od ljudi i počeo da odlazi na reku.

Kupio je mali splav i tamo provodio sve svoje slobodno vreme.

Gledanje u vodu pomagalo mu je da bar nakratko pročisti misli, ali drvored topola na suprotnoj obali nije mu davao mira.

Topole su bile jednake visine, kao da su im krošnje izravnate lenjirom.

„Stotinu stabala ne može da raste tako pravilno", mislio je. „To je neko morao da uradi. Ali ko? "

Nije imao odgovor.

Uostalom, nije imao odgovore ni na mnogo važnija pitanja.

Jednog popodneva dok se sunčao na svom splavu, u vazduhu je ugledao svoju sjajnožutu vizitkartu.

Lelujala se i prevrtala, ponirala i uzdizala se, iako nije bilo ni daška vetra.

Začuđeno ju je gledao kako leti, a zatim naglo nestaje u visinama, usisana promajom kakvu u životu nije osetio.

## Epiphany, a Small Demonstration of Power

As the years passed, he became more and more resigned.

Since he had retired, he was especially troubled by the question of God, the thought of transience, the impossibility of finding out what happens "after."

Slowly he began to separate himself from people and began going to the river.

He bought a small houseboat, and there he spent all his free time.

Watching the water helped him to clear his thoughts, at least briefly, but the row of poplar trees on the opposite bank didn't give him any peace.

The poplars were the same height, as if the treetops were evened out by a ruler.

"A hundred trees cannot grow that regularly," he thought. "Someone had made that happen. But who?"

He had no answer.

Besides, he had no answers to even more important questions.

One afternoon while he was sunning on his houseboat, he spotted his shiny yellow business card in the air.

It swayed and twirled, plummeting and then rising, even though there wasn't even a trace of wind.

Astonished, he watched it fly, then suddenly disappear into the heights, sucked up by a draft the likes of which he had never before experienced.

## **Spiritualni život**

Nije radio ništa ozbiljno.
Hranio je vrapce na prozoru, golubove u parku.
Noću je izlazio u šetnju i često stajao pred izlozima knjižara.

Ništa od toga nije bilo stvarno.
Tako je zamišljao sebe u trenucima predaha između dva posla.
Kao nadaren programer lako je nalazio zaposlenje i za sve veće honorare radio sve ozbiljnije projekte.
Konačno, dobio je ponudu iz inostranstva da bude deo tima za izradu nastavka jedne veoma popularne video-igre.
Iznosu na svom bankovnom računu mogao je dodati još jednu nulu, ali nije bio u stanju da se koncentriše na tako zahtevan posao.
Ponudu je morao da odbije.
Misli mu je zaposedao nezaposlen stariji brat koji je pisao pesme i živeo od milostinje najbližih.
(Brat je ponekad hranio vrapce na prozoru, golubove u parku, noću šetao od izloga do izloga knjižara u potrazi za novim izdanjima poezije.)
Život njegovog brata činio mu se mnogo smislenijim od sopstvenog, pa je sve svoje slobodno vreme trošio zamišljajući kako i sam besposličari i piše stihove.
Bila je to prolazna maštarija budućeg milionera.
Privremena blokada, bagovanje softvera.
Pad antivirusnog sistema.

# Spiritual Life

He didn't do anything seriously.
He was feeding sparrows on the window sill, or pigeons in the park.
At night he would go for a walk and often find himself standing in front of bookstore windows.

None of that was real.
That is how he imagined himself during his break between two jobs.
As a talented programmer he found jobs easily and for much higher pay he would work on even more serious projects.
Finally, he got an offer from abroad to be a part of a team creating the sequel to a very popular video game.
He could add another zero to his bank account, but he was unable to concentrate on such a demanding job.
He had to decline the offer to stay on.
His thoughts were preoccupied with his older unemployed brother who wrote poetry, living on charity of his immediate family.
(His brother sometimes fed sparrows on the window sill, the pigeons in the park, at night he walked from bookstore window to bookstore window in search of new collections of poetry.)
His brother's life seemed much more meaningful to him than his own, so that all his own free time he spent imagining how he too could be idle and be writing poetry line by line.
This was just a passing phase in the life of a future millionaire.
A temporary blockout, a software bug.
An antivirus system crash.

## O uticaju razređenog vazduha na povređeno samoljublje

Posle deset godina priprema, bez učitelja, kondicionog trenera i pouzdanih vodiča, popeo se na svoju prvu planinu.

Nije bila naročito visoka, ali zbog njene velike udaljenosti mnogi su je izbegavali.

Bio je jedan od prvih na njenom vrhu.

Podvig je ponovio još dva puta.

Samouk, i bez sekundanata, osvojio je tri udaljena planinska vrha, svaki nešto viši od prethodnog.

To ga je ispunilo neverovatnim ponosom.

Zadovoljan, ali iscrpljen višegodišnjim naporima, odlučio se za predah.

Privremeno je odustao od alpinizma i vratio se svakodnevici.

Živeo je u garsonjeri i za novac ljudima gledao u karte.

Bio je to lagodan život, ali ljubav prema penjanju nije ga ostavljala na miru.

Potražio je kolege i našao ih kako se pentraju po lokalnim brdima.

Međusobno su se bodrili i ispomagali, a u trenucima odmora jeli čorbu iz istog kotlića i pekli kobasice u istoj vatri.

Javio im se i pitao ih kako im ide, ali oni su okrenuli glave.

Povređenog ponosa (ipak se on popeo na tri kakve-takve planine), odlučio je da im se više ne obraća.

Nastaviće da se penje sam, na svoju ruku, kao i do tada.

# About the Influence of Diluted Air on the Injured Self

After ten years of preparation, without a teacher, a fitness trainer or reliable guides, he climbed to the top of his first mountain.

It wasn't extremely high, but because of its remoteness, most avoided it.

He was one of the first to reach its peak.

He repeated his achievement twice more.

Self-taught, and without an assistant, he conquered two far-away mountain peaks, each higher than the other.

That filled him with immense pride.

Satisfied, but exhausted by years of effort, he decided to take a break.

He quit alpine climbing temporarily and returned to everyday life.

He lived in a studio apartment and for money he read cards for people.

It was an easy living, but his love of climbing wouldn't leave him in peace.

He looked for colleagues and found them climbing local hills.

They mutually supported and helped each other, and during leisure time they ate soup from the same cauldron and roasted sausage on the same fire.

He called out to them and asked them how they were doing, but they turned their heads away.

With wounded pride (he had after all climbed three pretty high mountains), he decided not to contact them anymore.

He will continue to climb on his own as he had done before.

But he wasn't strong enough for the highest mountains

Za najviše planine nije bio dovoljno jak i zato je izvrnuo pravila igre: osvajaće planine „odozgo".

Počeo je da šije padobran s kojim će se, direktno iz aviona, spuštati na najviše, samo pogledu dostupne vrhove.

Nije znao da su upravo na tim, najvišim tačkama odavno izgrađene vile, bazeni i parkinzi.

I da nepozvani gosti nisu dobrodošli.

any more, so he turned the rules of the game: he was going to capture mountains "from the top down."

He began to sew a parachute with which he would descend directly from a plane onto the highest peaks, the ones only accessible by sight.

He didn't know that on those exact, highest points, were villas, swimming pools and parking lots, all built a long time ago.

Nor that uninvited guests were not welcome.

## Uskrsnuća-nestajanja

Pokušavao je da se priseti nekih godina, ali nije uspevao.
Nekakva beličasta izmaglica, nalik snu, kao da je prekrila skoro čitavu njegovu prošlost.
Zar je prespavao svo to vreme?
Gde su otišla sva ta lica, svi ti događaji?
Za svoju „uspavanost" krivio je otrovnu neonsku mesečinu, mali grad gde se rodio, u kome se vreme zaustavljalo-milelo.
Skoro da se pretvorio u stablo kada su ga spasili.
Posle jedne velike pijanke strpali su ga u auto, odvezli u prestonicu i ostavili da živi tamo.
U početku je imao utisak da se privremeno preselio, kako se nalazi na produženom letovanju s kojeg će jednog dana morati nazad.
Posmatrao je ulice, parkinge, autobuska stajališta i okretnice, solitere, blokove, prolaznike, i pokušavao da zamisli svoj život u novom okruženju za desetak godina.
Nakratko, bio je zbunjen, razočaran, nostalgičan.
Brzo se pribrao.
Imao je dovoljno dokaza da veruje kako život tek počinje.

## Resurrections-Disappearances

He was trying to remember prior years, but failed.

A sort of white fog, resembling a dream, seemed to have covered his entire past.

Had he slept through all that time?

Where had all those faces, all those events gone?

For his "sleepiness" he blamed the poisonous, neon moonlight, a small city where he was born, where time had stopped or was barely moving, plodding along.

He had almost turned into a tree, when they saved him.

After finding him in a huge drunken stupor, they put him in a car and drove him to the capitol, leaving him to live there.

At first he had a feeling that he had moved there temporarily, as if on an extended summer vacation from which one day he would have to return.

He observed the streets, parking lots, bus stops and roundabouts, skyscrapers, blocks of buildings, and passersby and then tried to imagine life in these new surroundings in ten years.

In short he was disoriented, disappointed, nostalgic.

Quickly he took a hold of himself.

Hadn't he enough proof to believe life was just beginning?

## Tajanstvena plavuša

Svetlucave katarke solitera pridržavale su umorno, oklembešeno nebo.

Stajao je na terasi, s laktovima oslonjenim na metalnu ogradu, kada je iza sebe osetio dim.

Okrenuo se i ugledao svoju sobu u plamenu.

Vatra je zahvatila zavese i brzo se širila na knjige iz biblioteke.

Odmah je znao da sanja – u kući nije imao knjiga.

Pljunuo je preko ograde, okrenuo se i zakoračio kroz vatreni zid.

Našao se u baru s crvenim plišanim stolicama i šankom od mahagonijuma.

Podigao je ruku i od barmena poručio piće.

Klateći se na visokim potpeticama prišla mu je plavuša s frizurom vamp boginje iz holivudskih noar filmova pedesetih.

Stala je pred njega i rekla:

„Čoveka je lako razotkriti. Samo ga pitaj šta želi."

Zbunjeno se nasmešio i upro prstom u nju:

„Ti si Rebeka, zar ne?..."

Tu se probudio.

Obično posle buđenja nije bio dobre volje, ali prožimao ga je pomalo neodređen, treperavi osećaj zadovoljstva pri pomisli na noćašnji san.

Čitavog dana razmišljao je o tome kako bi bilo lepo da se ponovo nađe u istom snu.

Provocirala ga je misteriozna plavuša.

Ko je ona?

Kako se zove?

## The Mysterious Blonde

The shiny masts of skyscrapers were supporting the tired, drooping sky.

He stood on the terrace with his elbows leaning onto the metal fence, when suddenly he smelled smoke behind him.

He turned around and saw that his room was on fire.

The fire had caught the curtains and was slowly spreading to the books from the library.

He knew immediately that he was dreaming—he didn't have any books in his house.

He spat across the fence, turned around and stepped into the firewall.

Then he found himself in a bar with red velvet chairs and a mahogany counter.

He lifted his hand to order a drink from the bartender.

A blonde swaying with her high heels, with vamp, goddess hair from Hollywood Film Noir movies approached him.

Standing before him, she said,

"It's easy to reveal a man. Just ask him what he wants."

Confused he smiled and pointed a finger at her.

"You're Rebecca, aren't you?"

That's when he woke up.

Usually after waking up, he was not in a good mood, but this time he was infused with a somewhat undefined fluttering feeling of pleasure as he recalled last night's dream.

All day long he thought about how great it would be to be back in the same dream again.

The mysterious blonde had provoked him.

Who was she?

What was her name?

Šta je želela da mu kaže?

Nije verovao da je moguće svesno nastaviti prekinuti san, ali intenzivno je mislio na njega u nadi kako mu to možda pomogne kada bude zaspao.

A onda je iznenada shvatio.

Plavuša je bila u pravu.

Stajao je na sredini sobe s visoko podignutim rukama.

Pobednički osećaj strujao mu je žilama do čvrsto stisnutih pesnica.

What did she want to tell him?

He didn't believe it was possible consciously to continue the broken dream, but he thought about it intensely in the hope that it would help him when he fell asleep.

But then he suddenly figured it out.

The blonde was right.

He stood in the middle of the room with both arms raised high.

A victorious feeling flowed through his veins into his tightly clenched fists.

## Misterije organizma

Upoznali su se na snimanju reklame za jastuk od memorijske pene.
Iako je imala snažna ramena i nabildovane udove, što nikako nije voleo kod žena, odmah se zaljubio u nju.

... Prva scena: ona spava na tom „savršenom jastuku".
Glas iz ofa govori kako se zbog pravilnog položaja vrata ostvaruje bolja cirkulacija krvi u glavi.
Budi se naspavana i dobro raspoložena.
Baca pogled na jastuk i nežno ga potapše.
U kadar ulazi on i izgovara brojeve telefona na koje se može naručiti taj „neverovatan proizvod" za miran i zdrav san.
Ona gužva jastuk koji se brzo vraća u prvobitno stanje.
Glas spikera kaže da je jastuk izrađen od specijalnog materijala koji je izumela NASA (uobičajeni trik).
On još jednom u kameru ponovi iste brojeve telefona.
Ona i on se zadovoljno osmehuju...

Po završenom snimanju nameravao je da joj predloži izlazak na piće, možda zatraži broj telefona.
Ali, kao i mnogo puta pre toga, u ključnom trenutku, obuzela ga je iznenadna, parališuća slabost.
Nemoćno ju je gledao kako se ljubazno pozdravlja sa svima iz filmske ekipe, seda u svoj mali japanski automobil i odlazi.
Sledeća tri meseca, svake noći ostajao je budan kako bi

## Mysteries of the Organism

He met her at the filming of a commercial for a memory foam pillow.

Even though she had strong shoulders and muscular arms and legs, which he didn't like in women, he still fell in love with her immediately.

...Scene one: she sleeps on that "perfect pillow."

The voice from offstage says that the supported position of the neck causes better circulation of blood in the head.

She wakes up having had a good sleep and rises in a good mood.

She glances at the pillow, then gently taps it.

At this point, he enters the frame and recites the phone numbers where one could order that "amazing product" for a peaceful and healthy sleep.

She fluffs the pillow which quickly returns to its original form.

The voice of the speaker says that the pillow has been made from a special material created by NASA (the usual trick).

He repeats the phone numbers into the camera once more.

She and he smile, satisfied...

After the filming ended, he intended to ask her out for a drink, maybe to ask her for her phone number.

But, as often before, in key moments, he was struck by a sudden, paralyzing weakness.

He helplessly looked at her as she was saying goodbye to everyone from the film crew, got into her small Japanese car, and left.

For the next three months every night he would stay up so

na kablovskom TV kanalu specijalizovanom za komercijani program mogao da vidi reklamu koju su snimili.

    Gledao je zanesen u njenu dugu negovanu kosu, u njen blistav osmeh, u njeno čvrsto telo oblikovano svakodnevnim posetama teratani.

    Vremenom, sve više je počela da mu smeta njena robustna, gotovo muška konstitucija.

    Odlučio je da „raskine" s njom.

    Na istom TV kanalu, upoznao je dugonogu, vitku meleskinju iz reklame za sobni bicikl.

    Nije mu bilo važno to što meleskinja živi u Americi.

    Bila je njegov tip.

he could watch her on the special cable channel in the ad they had filmed together.

He watched, mermerized by her long, groomed hair, her glistening smile, her fit body shaped by those daily gym sessions.

But in time, her robust, almost male frame began to bother him more and more.

He decided to "break it off" with her.

On the same TV channel, he met a long legged, slim mulatto woman from the exercise bike ad.

It didn't bother him that the mulatto lived in the US.

She was more his type.

## Nesigurnosti

Nalakćen na šank posmatrao je devojku s crvenim pramenom koji joj je padao preko leve polovine lica.
Okretala je narukvicu oko tankog zgloba i izgledala veoma usamljena.

(Reći će joj kako ljudi koji se ne smeju nisu lepi.
Ona će se na to verovatno nasmejati.)

O sebi nije imao šta da joj kaže.
Nekako se održavao na površini, bez izgleda da snažnije zavesla prema uspehu.

(Primetiće nešto u vezi s njenom frizurom.
Ona će ga možda pitati zašto nosi dva broja veći sako.)

Nije bio rečit, baratao je s premalo citata.
Namestio je umorni smešak, kao da mu je dosadno.

(Pitaće je kako se zove.
Ona će verovatno uzvratiti pitanjem – zašto on to želi da zna.)

Imao je petnaest kada mu je otac u jednoj šetnji savetovao da ne razmišlja o kosmosu ili o bogu.
„Razmišljaj o ženama", rekao mu je tada.

(Staće pred nju.
Ona će prestati da okreće narukvicu oko zgloba.)

## Uncertainties

Leaning with his elbows on the bar, he was looking at a girl with a red streak in her hair which fell over the left side of her face.

She was turning her bracelet around her thin wrist and looked very lonely.

(Maybe he could tell her how people who don't smile are not pretty.

That probably would make her smile.)

He had nothing to tell her about himself.

Somehow he had managed to float by without a likelihood of ever reaching more powerful paths towards success.

(He could mention something about her hair.

She would perhaps ask him why he's wearing a jacket that is two sizes too big for him.)

He wasn't eloquent, he could cite very few quotes.

He put on a tired smile, as if he were bored.

(He'd ask her what her name is.

She'd probably answer by asking why he wants to know.)

He was fifteen when during a walk with his father, the old man advised him not to think about the cosmos or god.

"Think about women," he told him then.

(He would stand before her.

She would stop turning the bracelet around her wrist.)

Duboko je udahnuo i krenuo ka devojci s crvenim pramenom.

Već posle prvog koraka našao se u potpunom mraku.

He took a deep breath and began to walk toward the girl with the red streak.

After his first step, he already found himself in complete darkness.

## Učiteljevim stopama

Mučile su ga nesnosne migrene.
Kao po pravilu, počinjale su u petak popodne i prestajale u nedelju uveče.
Vikende je provodio ležeći u zamračenoj sobi.
Preko nedelje rešavao je probleme na poslu.
Firma mu je bila u blokadi.
Poverioci su ga svakodnevno zvali ili lično dolazili u kancelariju.
Od banke je dobio i treće upozorenje da će mu uzeti stan zbog neizmirenih rata kredita.
Bivša žena mu je pretila tužbom zbog kašnjenja s alimentacijom.
Nevolje su se gomilale.
Tonuo je sve dublje dok jednog dana nije odlučio da proda sve što poseduje: polovinu otplaćene nekretnine, vikendicu, automobil, nameštaj, kućne aparate...
Za dva meseca nameru je sproveo u delo.
Podmirio je dugove kod banke i poverilaca, ugasio firmu, iselio se iz stana.
Ono što nije uspeo da proda poklonio je *Crvenom krstu* i sirotištu.
Odlučio je da postane beskućnik.
Migrene su prestale čim je počeo da spava pod otvorenim nebom.
Budio se svež, poletan, u cik zore počinjao je da pešači.
Saznanje da ništa ne poseduje ispunjavalo ga je spokojem.

## In the Teacher's Footsteps

He suffered from unbearable migraines.

As a rule they began on Friday afternoons and stopped by Sunday evenings.

He spent the weekends in a darkened room.

During the week he solved problems at work.

His company went bankrupt.

His creditors were calling him every day or personally coming to his office.

He got a third warning from the bank that they would take his apartment because of his unpaid mortgage.

His ex-wife threatened to sue him for late alimony.

His troubles were piling up.

He was drowning deeper and deeper, until one day he decided to sell everything he possessed: half of the paid-off property, his country house, the car, his furniture, his appliances....

In two months, he managed to take care of his debts.

He paid off his bank and creditors, closed down his business, moved out of his apartment.

What he did not manage to sell, he gave to the Red Cross and the orphanage.

He decided to become homeless.

His migraines stopped as soon as he began to sleep under an open sky.

He would wake up refreshed, joyful— as he would begin walking at dawn.

The knowledge that he possessed nothing filled him with serenity.

## Strujanje misli u kupatilu

Čekao je prijatelja da dođe kako bi zajedno krenuli na utakmicu.

Fudbalski tim za koji su navijali igrao je odlučujući kvalifikacioni meč protiv veoma jakog inostranog rivala.

Prognoze za dalji prolaz voljenog kluba bile su pesimističke.

Ušao je u kupatilo da se istušira i obrije.

Stajao je u kadi obuzet crnim slutnjama; ispadanje, kraj...

Misli o smrti i samoubistvu nadovezale su se na loše predosećanje o ishodu utakmice.

Trgnuo se.

Zašto uopšte razmišlja o tim stvarima?

I odkud te mračne misli, njemu koji je tako veseo, pun života.

Počeo je da se brije.

Lavina je krenula ponovo.

... Oko njega su jurili superbrzi električni vozovi puni navijača.

… U martinkama i s bejzbol palicom skrivenom ispod jakne šunjao se ulicama u potrazi za strancima sa šalovima protivničkog tima.

… Bacao je kamenice na zapaljene policijske automobile.

Prijatelj ga je zatekao u kupatilu kako razdragan peva:

*Jedan vojnik kreće u rat!*

*U rat! U rat! U rat!*

*Gladan je, gladan borbe.*

Prijatelj ništa nije posumnjao.

Stanje je bilo redovno.

## The Streaming of Thoughts in the Bathroom

He was waiting for a friend, so they could go to the match together.

Their favorite soccer team, was about to play a deciding, qualifying match against a very tough foreign rival.

Predictions for the further advancement of their beloved team were pessimistic.

He went into the bathroom to shower and shave.

He stood in the bathtub, overcome with dark thoughts; the likelihood of dropping out, the end...

Thoughts of death and suicide followed his premonitions about the match's outcome.

He shuddered.

Why was he even thinking about these things?

And where did those dark thoughts come from, for him who is so joyful, so full of life?

He began to shave.

The avalanche of thoughts started again.

...Around him swirled speeding electric trains filled with fans.

...In Doc Martins and just one bat hidden under his jacket, he went out to sneak around streets in search of foreigners with scarves of the opposing team's colors.

...Next thing he knew he was throwing rocks at burning police cars.

But his friend found him in the bathroom, happily singing:
*A soldier is going to war.*
*To war! To war! To war!*
*Starving, starving for a fight.*
His friend suspected nothing.
This behavior was ordinary.

## Edip, na rubu ponora

Bio je razveden, bez dece.

Svakog popodneva, nakon posla, obilazio je nepokretnu majku.

Gurao ju je u kolicima, vodio u šetnje i na izlete.

Nalazio je i plaćao patronažne sestre da dvadeset i četiri časa brinu o njoj.

Nije imao srca da je smesti u dom.

Nije imao srca ni da joj kaže kako mu je glava postala pokvareni bojler iz koga kaplje voda.

(Čuo je glasove kako mu šapuću: „Zakrpi rupu na kazanu... Očisti kamenac...")

Odbijao je i samu pomisao da poseti lekara.

Ko će brinuti o majci?

Stanje mu se pogoršavalo.

Počeo je da guta lekove, najobičnije tablete protiv glavobolje.

Nadao se da će glasovi koje čuje brzo utihnuti.

Jedne noći sanjao je kako strada u automobilskoj nesreći i ostaje paralizovan.

Majka mu dolazi u posetu i njih dvoje, svako u svojim invalidskim kolicima, igraju košarku.

Probudio se srećan.

Učinilo mu se da su to najlepši trenuci provedenih s majkom, još od detinjstva.

Posle mnogo vremena, izašao je iz stana sa smeškom na usnama.

## Oedipus, on the Brink of an Abyss

He was divorced, without children.

Every afternoon, after work he went to visit his bed-ridden mother.

He pushed her in her wheelchair, took her out for walks and picnics.

He found and paid nurses to take care of her twenty-four hours a day.

He just didn't have the heart to put her in a nursing home.

He just didn't have the heart to tell her that his own head had become a broken water boiler leaking in gallons.

(He heard voices whispering to him, "Fix the hole in the boiler…Scrape off the limescale …")

He rejected even the very possibility of going to see a doctor.

Who'd take care of his mother?

His condition worsened.

He began to swallow medication, the simplest headache pills.

He hoped the voices he heard would soon disappear.

One night he dreamt he was in a car accident and had become paralyzed.

His mother came to visit him at the hospital, and the two of them, each in their wheelchair, played basketball.

He woke up elated.

It seemed to him these were the best moments spent with his mother, the best since childhood.

After a long time had passed, he walked out of his apartment with a smile on his face.

Tog dana nakon posla, umesto kod majke, otišao je u zoološki vrt.

Sedeo je na klupi ispred kaveza s leopardom, i čitavo popodne zurio u njega.

That day after work, instead of going to his mother's, he went to the zoo.

He sat on the bench in front of the leopard cage and for the entire afternoon stared at it.

## Jedan život, jedna karijera

Imao je mnogo sreće u genetskom ruletu.
Priroda je njegovu konstituciju proizvela savršeno poput nemačkih automobila, dugotrajnih i pouzdanih.
Najvažniji savet dobio je još kao desetogodišnjak.
Crveni patuljak iz dvorišta, reko mu je:
„Ne smeš da postaneš žardinjera u slabo prometnoj ulici."
Iako tek dečačić, razumeo je značenje tih reči.
Krenuo je oštro već u srednjoj školi:
Sumanuto je menjao ploče na gramofonu.
Čitao knjige koje su snažile misli.
Patikama nerazumno habao beton.
Nije mu bilo ni osamnaest kada je odlučio da se nikada ne zaposli.
I tu mu je dobro išlo.
Preskakao je neumoljive kazaljke jutra, odbijao da nosi odela i kravate, izbegavao burmu.
Godine su prolazile (novac je nekako pristizao), a on je živeo mnogo lagodnije i izgledao mnogo mlađe od svojih vršnjaka.
Dokolica mu je oslabila reflekse.
Postao je nepažljiv, pomalo rasejan.
Jedne zime, dok je čistio sneg na parkingu ispred zgrade, udario ga je autobus.
Prikovan za postelju, ugledao je crvenog patuljka, onog istog od pre mnogo godina.
Patuljak mu je prišao i šapnuo na uho:

## One Life, One Career

He was very lucky at the genetics roulette.

Nature had manufactured his body's constitution perfectly, like that of a German car, durable and reliable.

The best advice he had received was when he was ten years old.

The red gnome in the backyard told him,

"You cannot become a street planter box on a quiet street?"

Even though he was still a young boy, he understood what those words meant.

He was fierce even in high school.

He changed records on the record player as if possessed.

He read books that strengthen thoughts.

Manicly he pounded the concrete sidelwalk and wore out tennis shoes.

He wasn't even eighteen yet when he decided never to get a job.

He did well there.

He would jump over the unsettling hour hand of the mornings and patently refused to wear suits and ties, also avoided wearing the wedding ring.

Years passed by (the money somehow kept coming), and he lived a much easier fortunate life continuing to look much younger than other people his age.

But so much leisure weakened his reflexes.

He became less careful and more scatterbrained.

One winter while he was shoveling the snow in the parking lot, in front of his building, he was hit by a bus.

Confined to bed, he envisioned the red gnome, the same one from years ago.

The gnome approached him and whispered—

„Sve je moglo da bude drugačije, ništa nije moglo da bude drugačije."

Bile su to poslednje reči koje je čuo.

"Everything could have been different, nothing could have been different."

Those were the last words he heard.

## Demoni u bordelu

U prigušenom svetlu razaznao je demone kako lebde nad sofama.
Iste one prikaze zbog kojih je i izašao iz tog stana pre mnogo godina.
Pravio se da ih ne primećuje.
Prošao je pored njih zagledan u visoke tavanice požutele od duvanskog dima, u teške plišane zavese pune prašine, u poluraspadnut stilski nameštaj.
Ta rupa je zaista ličila na jeftin bordel.
Muvao se po stanu izbegavajući lisičja lica uramljena u žute i crne perike, svinjska lica s čašama u rukama.
Seo je na praznu želatinsku stolicu, a onda ugledao plavokosu striptizetu i premestio se do nje.
Nežno mu je prebacila ruku preko ramena i šaputala na uho o potrebi dokumentovanja sopstvenog života.
Osetio je strašan umor.
Glava mu je klonula u njeno krilo.
Najlonske čarape dodirivale su mu obraz dok je padao u san.
Probudila ga je užasna zvonjava.
Batler je stajao iznad njega, s telefonskom slušalicom u ispruženoj ruci.
„Vaša majka želi da vas čuje", rekao je.
Bez reči je prihvatio aparat, prekinuo vezu i krenuo napolje.
U hodniku je vladala gužva.
Dolazile su neke visoke zvanice.
Žene s šeširima i u dugačkim večernjim haljinama, gospoda u smokinzima i s leptir-mašnama koračali su odlučno po crvenom tepihu.

## Demons in the Brothel

In the dimmed light, he could make out demons floating above sofas.

They were the same apparitions which caused him to leave that apartment years before.

He pretended at first as if he he hadn't noticed them.

He passed by them staring at the high ceiling, yellowed from tobacco smoke, and into heavy velvet curtains full of dust and dilapidated antique furniture.

That hole really resembled a cheap brothel.

He moved around the apartment avoiding the sly fox-like faces framed by yellow and black wigs, pig faces with glasses in their hands.

He sat on a vacant gelatin chair, but then spotted a blonde stripper and moved next to her.

She gently put her arm around him and whispered into his ear about the urgency to document one's own life.

He felt terribly tired.

His head fell onto her lap.

Her nylon tights brushed his cheek as he was falling asleep.

He woke up to a loud bell ringing.

The butler stood above him with a phone in an outstretched hand.

"Your mother wants to speak to you, sir," he announced.

Without saying anything, he took the receiver, disconnected the line and left the room.

In the hallway things were busy.

Some high officials were arriving at that moment.

Women with hats and in long evening gowns, gentlemen in tuxedos with bow ties, promenaded confidently on the red carpet.

Vazduh je bežao ispred njihovih jakih parfema.
Blicevi su sevali.
Ljudi su uzbuđeno šaputali:
„Stiže upravni odbor *Udruženja sapunskih opera*!"
Probio se kroz uskomešanu gomilu, i nekako uspeo da izađe iz stana.
Spustio se na mezanin.
Naslonio se na zid i stavio slušalice na uši.
Začuo je meketavi glas svoje majke.
Pevala je neki svoj stari hit.
Odjednom, iz stana je pokuljao gusti crni dim.
Gužva pred vratima proključala je.
Umesto da beže, ljudi su se tukli da uđu unutra.
Zbunjeno je gledao u njihova ozarena, ushićena lica, dok su se gurali i laktali i krvnički udarali ne bi li se dočepali zapaljenog stana.
„Nešto se dešava ovde, ali ti ne znaš šta, zar ne, gospodine Džouns...", čuo je majku kako peva.
I tada se setio da odavno nije posetio svoj dom.

The air fled from the scene of the strong perfumes.

Flashbulbs were popping.

People were whispering with excited anticipation.

"The Soap Opera Association committee is arriving soon."

He managed to get through the turbulent crowd, and somehow left the apartment.

He descendeed to the mezzanine.

Then he leaned into the wall and put on headphones.

He heard the sheep-like sound of his mother's voice.

She was singing some old classic.

Suddenly, black smoke poured out from the apartment.

In front of the door the mass of people began to boil.

Instead of running away, people fought each other to get back inside.

Confused, he examined their lit up, excited faces, while they pushed, elbowed and bludgeoned each other, so as to try to enter the flaming apartment.

"Something is happening here, but you don't know what it is, do you, Mr. Jones...," he heard his mother sing.

But then, he recalled he had not visited his home for years.

## Afterword

## Prose Poems of Zvonko Karanović: Portrait of a Mature, Rebelling Artist[1]

The Serbian poet, Zvonko Karanović, is primarily a lyrical, surreal poet, even though he has three novels, published before his most recent collections of prose poems, *Sleepwalkers on a Picnic* (2012), *Cages* (2013), *Golden Age* (2015) and *Beyond the Burning Forest* (2018). Since his fiction has been so successful, many Serbian critics believed he might give up on poetry altogether. Still, Karanović continues primarily to write poetry—his first love, even if it is often in the form of prose poetry, unusual for Serbia, the form itself being part of his rebellious streak. As a West-oriented artist, Karanović employs surreal images that mirror the despair in his country, Serbia. Authentic writing is too strong. His prose poems are a portrait of a mature artist who is clearly rebelling.

Karanović, born in Niš, Serbia in 1959, now lives and works

---

[1] From a paper delivered at the South Central Modern Langauge Association's annual conference's panel, Slavic and Eastern
European Languages and Literatures in Tulsa, OK on October 5, 2017.

in Belgrade as a freelance writer and, recently a small press publisher. He has worked as a journalist, editor, radio host, DJ, concert organizer, and owner of a music store for thirteen years. His four collections of free verse prior to his recent two works of prose poems include: *Blitzkrieg* (Samizdat, 1990), *Srebrni Surfer* (Niš: SKC, 1991), *Mama melanholija* (Belgrade: Prosveta, 1996), *Extravaganza* (Niš: Gradina, 1997), *Tamna magistrala* (Belgrade: Narodna Knjiga, 2001), and *Svlačenje* (Kraljevo: Povelja, 2004), as well as several books of selected poems. Some of his books have been translated into sixteen languages[1], and he has received Serbian literary awards for poetry and international fellowships. His work has also been anthologized, most significantly in the US, in *New European Poets* (Graywolf Press, 2008) and *Cat Painters: An Anthology of Contemporary Serbian Poetry* (Diálogos, 2016). His most recent collection, *It Was Easy To Set the Snow On Fire – Selected Poems* (Phoneme Media, 2016), translated into English by Ana Božičević, appeared in the US.

Even so, his novels have received most attention in Serbia. These books follow his prose project, a novel trilogy, *The Diary of Deserters*, comprised of the novels *More Than Zero* (2004), *Four Walls and the City* (2006), and *Three Snapshots of Victory* (2009), set in the period between 1998 and 2000, the trilogy chronicles the lives of three young urban men who, fighting for their beliefs, attempt to live freely in an unfree land, a prominent theme in his work. The trilogy is dedicated to Serbia's "lost generation," those who, in the 1990s, either left the country, perished in the new Balkan civil wars, or suffered social marginalization due to their cosmopolitan worldview.

---

1  English, French, German, Spanish, Italian, Polish, Ukrainian, Greek, Hungarian, Bulgarian, Macedonian, Slovenian, Slovakian, Czech, Albanian, Arabic...

What Serbian critics have expected him to do is to continue writing fiction. After all, like everywhere else, fiction pays in Serbia today, and poetry does not. But, Karanović is a devoted poet. From the start he has been rebellious, wants to do things differently.

I first met Karanović in May 2012 in Belgrade at the Serbian Writers Association, where I was working with Dubravka Djurić on co-editing, *Cat Painters: An Anthology of Contemporary Serbian Poetry*. As one of the writers in the anthology, he says, "In the beginning I was writing short poems, not longer than three or four lines. I was influenced by the Serbian translations of Whitman and Pound, classic anthologies of American poetry, but also of Beat poetry and underground poetry, New York School and Black Mountain poets, and underground poets." He also notes, "After coming back from the army in 1986, I started writing longer, narrative poems," and began publishing poems. Karanović was fascinated by American culture, "primarily by the beatniks, the San Francisco music and the comic books scene, pop art, the work of American underground authors from Bukowski to Hunter S. Thompson." He says he came to "love the Beats and American poetry accidentally through texts by and interviews with Bob Dylan and Patti Smith. Then a whole new world opened up for me" as "the Beats' antiwar sentiments, the destruction of all taboos, the openness to new experiences, the equality between life and writing, the spontaneity, the giving of all yourself had a huge impact on me."[1]

Most of his previous collections were in free verse, but he experimented quite a bit with the form even there, playing with the white space, and avoiding punctuation (but not capital

---

1   From an interview with Karanović by me, excerpts of which were published online in *WLT* (see: Works Cited)

letters); these new elements remain in his poetry to this day. He tries different points of view and unusually for Serbian poets, occasionally speaks from a female point of view. He says, "I didn't worry about the rules. Ginsberg used to say that everything that passes through the human mind is appropriate for poetry. [Ginsberg] destroyed the walls for me between 'high' and 'low' literature," adding, "All his poems are in essence some kind of stories, fragments of situations," so it's no wonder that Karanović would end up writing a collection of prose poems, as they are conduits to the narrative form.

Still, the socialist architecture and life seemed claustrophobic, so that Karanović's themes often address "alienation, loser-dom, loss of friendship, lost loves; drugs are openly mentioned; rock iconography is very present—therefore, it contained everything that did not exist on the domestic literary scene at that moment... against the Balkan tedium, read mostly by young people with a cosmopolitan orientation." But, the Balkan civil wars increased the desire for even more of the same. Many Serbs emigrated; he did not. But he captures "a desire for escape" in his earlier books like *Silver Surfer* (1991), "a direct consequence of the political events which preceded the military conflicts and the disintegration of the country. The end of the eighties brought an accumulation of dark clouds of nationalism, which culminated with the civil wars (1991–95)."

The poems that were included in *Silver Surfer* were created in the prewar period (1987–90), so that in some of them, between the lines, he captures "the atmosphere of the rising claustrophobia and premonition of the forthcoming dark times." He says, "The terror can only be overcome by witnessing it." So he doesn't run away, he confronts it head on in a poetry of witness. *Mama Melancholy* (1996) captures apocalyptic images and a wish for an escape from reality. He says that he fought the terror by endlessly watching movies, listening to music, and with self-destructive conduct. Unconsciously, he says he, "developed a technique of forgetting."

*Extravaganza* (1997) continues delving into the chaos in relation to the war and political unrest, but there are also glimpses of Karanović's personal life, "starting in 1996–97, marked with street protests and demonstrations against the [Milošević] regime, in which [he], too, was a participant." He says that, "After the end of the NATO intervention, in spring 2000, [he] realized that [he] felt incredibly tired from everything that [he] had experienced during the past decade. That's when [he] reached for Ginsberg's selected poems, which [he] hadn't been reading for years, and found the poem 'America,'"— interesting since his country was primarily bombed by the US lead NATO. But Ginsberg also protests his own country's wars and asks, "America when will we end the human war?/Go fuck yourself with the atom bomb" (Lines 4-5), (still relevant today) and that's how the two have found common ground. "And then in two days [he] wrote a response, another long poem [he] was going to title 'Serbia,' but which [he] ended up calling 'Great Fatigue,' a cynical and accusatory confession. Because of these openly anti-regime stances, [he] couldn't publish the poem anywhere. After the regime fell, [he] got an opportunity in 2001 to officially publish those two poems. That's how the collection *Dark Highway* (2001), came to be."

In that book, the speaker cannot handle anymore what's happening, so seems scared, tired, exhausted.... He says that, "The end of the nineties was marked by the 1999 NATO bombing of Serbia. Since the country was officially at war, total mobilization was declared, so that [he], like thousands of others, was drafted ([he]'d be jailed if [he] evaded it). [He] was in uniform for seventy-two days, but luckily in the rearguard, far away from the front and without firing a single bullet. The last days of the war, through the method of automatic writing and mind flow, [he] wrote the long poem 'Dark Highway' in order to find answers to all the absurdities that had been going on in the nineties." Clearly, his war experience could have ended tragically (as it has for so many artists in the past who, like himself, were forced to fight), but thankfully didn't.

The next collection, *Taking Off* (2004) was published in Serbia's democratic period. Karanović stopped writing for almost two years prior to that.... He says, "I was exhausted and tired of the decade of nightmares, and at the same time disgusted by looking at the 'winners' who sought a place and grabbed privilege in the new system...so now I was looking [at it all], in a slightly cynical and bitter tone from a distance. The title is another explicit stance about my poetry as some type of undressing, an emotional bearing of it all. Poetry has taught me that humans become the strongest precisely when they are the most hurt." After that collection of poems, he didn't write poetry for a while, and instead turned to his trilogy, *Diary of a Deserter* (2004–2009).

Following these works, came his first collection of prose poetry, *Sleepwalkers on a Picnic* (2012), this collection, then, *Cages* (2013). He says he, "found [his] inspiration in surrealism, to which [he] returned through classic and new achievements, but also through films by Buñuel and Lynch. [He] wanted to experiment with form as well." In this collection of poems in prose, "each poem can be treated as a [separate] story." Both collections have been reviewed positively in the press in Serbia and the first has won the Biljana Jovanović Award. This is very avant-garde work for Serbia, resembling Arthur Rimbaud's famous collection, *A Season in Hell,* which Karanović alludes to. Prose poetry looks like prose on the page, is in paragraphs rather than verse, but may contain the characteristics of poetry, such as poetic meter, language play, and a focus on images rather than narrative, plot, and character. Critic, Goran Lazičić says that, "perhaps these two are just the beginning of his new cycle, which may be continued." He continues to say that, even though, "his novel trilogy's success has surpassed the author's previous poetic reputation," one would expect that Karanović would continue in "that genre and leave behind poetry as a youthful initiation into one's writing career." But, Lazičić adds that, "the year he published his third novel, his collected poems, *Box Set* (2009) came out, as well as the fact that his poems appeared in two important Serbian anthologies of poetry in which he is represented as a leading poet of his generation," therefore implying that Karanović may, in fact, never return to fiction.

Another critic, Vladimir Arsenić, in his "Portraits of the Artist in Rebellion," points out "poetry in prose is quite a rarity in today's literature [in Serbia] that comes from the 19th century and most famously from Baudelaire's *Paris Spleen* collection." "This type of poetry is not popular in Serbian literature," says Arsenić. It's another way of rebelling against the tradition." Arsenić says that Karanović "leans towards…the neo avant-garde tradition of Vujica Resin Tucić, Vladimir Kopicl and Vojislav Despotov[1]" Arsenić says that, "Since he has come onto the scene, he has been a leader of a rebellion against the status quo that has prevailed. Since then he has been a poet many younger poets, like Miloš Živanović and Siniša Tucić, look up to." Arsenić says that *Sleepwalkers on a Picnic* is "the best book Karanović has written so far" and "a definitive move away from the hold of Serbian poetry. Karanović refuses any type of belonging."

---

1 Thee poet leaders of the avant-garde movement in poetry from the city of Novi Sad.

*Mesečari na Izletu* [*Sleepwalkers on a Picnic*] contains forty-one poems each being mostly one to two pages in length with short paragraphs comprised of one to two sentences each. These poems are all persona poems. The collection begins with an epigraph from James Tate, about a lost man who stumbles upon a new area in a city. As we begin, a man is talking to his mother, or rather a voice of his long dead mother, in a room filled with strippers in high heels who try to strangle him with a phone cord, while he gets an erection and helps them to strangle him. Sounds like a masochistic wet dream or nightmare. In the midst of this the "mother" is giving him advice about writing and art. Freud might have something to say about this! The book is filled with dreams, a lot of eroticism combined with death. Vladimir Arsenić in his review of this book, says that the first poem "In a Hotel Room" represents a clash between the dominant poetry and himself.

Dragana V. Todoreskov, another critic, says that he criticizes society, "through introspection looking at the shameful, obscure human being, unable to resist the whirlwind of war, sanctions, social misery, and moral crushing, of that gray and depressing atmosphere which only leads to denial and self-denial." His speaker "who is obsessed with the female body" is "depressingly alone and thoughtful," she says, and in him one can see a gentle, hypersensitive being, in whom poetry and music, especially rock and roll, really live."

Several poems are in female voices, as in, "In Spring with Love in Full Swing" (16-17), some in dialogue form as in "In the Literature Wilderness of Poetry" (35-37), many about art and literature as in "Literature and Violence" (42), some as mysterious chronicles as in "Chronicle of a Preset Disappearance" (48-49) or "Poetry for Everyone's Home." The latter turns out to be an ars poetica which includes a free verse poem within a prose poem about a man in his fifties who writes a poem after a long time; once a woman finds it and throws herself at him hoping to spend time with him till he dies....as "she planned to live forever" (55). But, then there are poems that express the opposite of this positive mood, as in "In the teacher's footsteps," about a man with migraines, who suffers from depression, divorce, and losing an apartment due to not paying his mortgage payments. He then sells everything he owns in a day and becomes homeless. Then his migraines stop, and he begins to "think of existence, god, the ruthless fight for material things" (79). Karanović, here is giving us some social commentary about materialism. Since he didn't own anything the man is finally satisfied, and redeemed.

This collection is about a man, an artist, with obvious psychological problems and at times seems like a Godard movie, or a Kafka short story. He alludes to other writers from Portugal, and Italy. In this collection we are on the edge of a nightmare. Each setting, poem after poem, is an apocalyptic urban landscape full of obscure characters, not unlike in the movies of David Lynch. The lonely poet is trying to find his place amongst those greats he refers to—from Bob Dylan, to Gotfried Benn.

Written after UN sanctions against Serbia, after the Yugoslavian civil war, and after the 1999 NATO bombings, these poems express an anti-Milošević, pro-Democrat position, as Karanović proves himself a rebellious poet whose images we see here are fantastic, grotesque, yet full of symbolism. Reading the poems is like reading Baudelaire or Rimbaud, but also like the surrealists James Tate and the Serbian American, Charles Simic. But, Karanović goes even further, it seems... A human is not a machine, he seems to be saying. He has an irrational side with his imagination, dreams, magic, myths, utopian ideals, dangerous, perhaps, but equally liberating, giving full ride to the oldest of human tendencies—erased by the rules dictated by modern society.

The next collection, *Kavezi* [*Cages*], like *Sleepwalkers on a Picnic*, also a surreal prose poetry collection, has also been conceptualized as a loose novel (psycho-drama), as the picture of Serbia it portrays becomes clear in the end. *Cages* has forty-three poems. It is "a psychedelic love story, a nightmarish perverted tale," he says. In the prologue and epilogue appear two lovers with very strange names, Žicoliki, a man, and Pticolika, a woman, representing a sort of parody of the gothic novel. They wish to escape reality, fly away for a holiday, but are in a cage prepared just for them. But, here's no escape from madness. The main characters are a journalist/ poet, Žak, and his female critic. The poet optimist's wife doesn't allow him to write poetry, constantly provoking him to kill her as she is unable to commit suicide herself, no matter that she wishes to die.

Critic, Goran Lazičić, in his review of *Cages*, "Sloboda među rešetkama" [Freedom inside Cages], says that the main characters in *Cages* are negative, evil, angels, [who] finally, in the end, go to Berlin, where they plan to mix business with pleasure." He says that, "He cannot be sentimental in the 21st century... can he not hear the absurdity of the words," so he is painting a picture of social reality of contemporary Serbia and its literature. The scenography and atmosphere of the cages is the darkness, but surrounding it are halogen discos. He creates a new bizarre world with the main characters sitting on a fluorescent red sofa mouth and a huge tarantula which appear all over the book. *Cages* are representative of the post transitional social realities of Serbia. Models, de facto prostitutes, vulgarity and materialism—that's where Karanović places the Serbian scene. There are certain episodes in which the protagonists appear in reality TV programs in which people have swapped places with birds. It's interesting that both of his original book covers look very similar, as if they're connected. However the first book, has one male protagonist and is not as connected, while the second book is more closely connected.

So what he's trying to say is that he is clearly aware of his own position in Serbian poetry. On the one hand, the mother in the poem, may represent the language he writes in, a parent from whom he cannot escape. The strippers are trying to strangle him, and he helps them to do so. He cannot run away from either side, yet nothing can stop the urge to do so, given what the speaker is experiencing. Authentic writing is too strong. It's a portrait of a mature artist who is clearly rebelling.

Mileta Aćimović Ivkov, says that in the *Sleepwalkers*, Karanović is showing a representation of "an anti-hero of our time." He says, "printing books of poems today is a joke," because obviously society is only interested in profit. In *Cages*, in a poem, "She Made Up Her Mind in the Beginning," he shows a critic as a monkey on a chain, not writing what she really thinks. This reminds me of Voltaire's work, especially, *Candide*, with its criticism of so many levels of society. What he is saying is that, "poetry is the highest form of responsibility," and that "a human being deserves heaven." Karanović, in other words, is not a sell-out. He will not create something just so he can make money. His morality will not allow it.

He constantly, whenever I see him, says that he wants to withdraw from society. But like all of us, he is a social being, and isolation would be incredibly difficult to achieve. But, instead of becoming a monk or a hermit, he simply must be true to his art and obey it. He chooses to do what his art asks of him, not to give into what society wants from him. That's the message of this collection. Poetry must not disappear into darkness, and neither will he. He fights a similar thing to Baudelaire's *ennui*[1] in his time, as well as Pound, Kafka, Ginsberg, Voltaire in theirs–to whom Karanović looks up as his predecessors. Now it is clear that younger poets are already also following Karanović himself.

---

1   *Ennuui*—a feeling of listlessness and dissatisfaction arising from a lack of occupation or excitement (synonyms: annoyance, despair, boredom, tedium, listlessness, lethargy…).

## Works Cited

Aćimović Ivkov, Mileta. "Zatamljena Mesečina." Niš: *Gradina*, no. 55-56-56.

Arsenić, Vladimir. "Portret Umetnika u Pobuni: Zvonko Karanović, *Mesečari na izletu* (Belgrade: LOM, 2012)" http://www.e-novine.com/kultura/kultura-knjige/72810-Portret-umetnika-pobuni.html

Karanović, Zvonko. *Cages*, 2013 (book of poems) May 2014. http://www.worldliteraturetoday.org/2014/may-august/kavezi-zvonko-karanovic#.VASftqN32So

—Interview for WLT with Biljana D. Obradović, "Rebel with a Cause in Serbia: A Conversation with Zvonko Karanović." Oct 2012. http://www.worldliteraturetoday.org/2013/may/rebel-cause-serbia-conversation-zvonko-karanovic-biljana-d-obradovic#.UgjOFn__SMU

—*Kavezi*. [*Cages*]. Belgrade: LOM, 2013.

—*Mesečari na izletu*. [*Sleepwalkers on a Picnic*]. Belgrade: LOM, 2012.

Ginsberg, Allen. "America." *Collected Poems: 1947-1980*. New York: Harper & Row, Publishers, 1984.

Lazičić, Goran. "Sloboda Među Rešetkama." http://agoncasopis.com/Broj_26/o%20poeziji/1-lazicic_kavezi.html

Stojković, Dušan. "Poezija Budućnosti." Kragujevac: *Koraci*, no. 4-6; 2014 https://issuu.com/nbkg/docs/korac4

Todoreskov, Dragana. "Kavezi: Psihonautika na muško-ženski način." *Književni magazin*. no. 154-157, Belgrade: Apr.-Jul. 2014.

# Notes

"In a Hotel Room": *Elastic band*—in Serbia kids (mostly girls) used to play a game with long elastic bands which they jump over.

"Sudden Events in the Museum of Memories": *A Season in Hell (Une Saison en Enfer)*—by French writer Arthur Rimbaud is an extended prose poem written and published in 1873. The book had a considerable influence on later artists and poets, including the Surrealists.

"About Rain and the End of Love": *Godard*—Jean-Luc Godard (French b.1930) is a French-Swiss film director, screenwriter and film critic. He is often identified with the 1960s French film movement *La Nouvelle Vague*, or "New Wave." Godard's films have inspired many directors including Martin Scorsese, Quentin Tarantino, Brian De Palma, Robert Altman, Jim Jarmusch, Bernardo Bertolucci, and Pier Paolo Pasolini. *Classical music on the radio*—in ex-Yugoslavia when there was a day of mourning all (government run) radio stations played only classical music all day.

"Commissar": *Commisar*—an officer of the Communist Party responsible for political education and organization.

"The Metamorphosis": *The Metamorphosis*—a novella by the same title by Franz Kafka was first published in 1915. It has been called one of the seminal works of fiction of the 20th century. The story begins with a traveling salesman, Gregor Samsa, waking to find himself transformed (metamorphosed) into a large, monstrous insect-like creature.

"Decisiveness of Middle Age": *Assam*—bold black tea from the Assam region of India. Assam tea is known for a deep, burgundy-red cup and pungent flavor.

"About Youth and the Things that Should Be Truthful": *A black ribbon*—placed over photos of those who have died recently and carried in funeral processions; also worn by the immediate family on their clothes, especailly if not wearing the traditional mourning black clothing for at least 40 days after the death of a a loved one in Serbia. This way people are aware they are mourning and respect their loss. *Seppuku*— sometimes referred to as *hara-kiri*, "abdomen/belly cutting," a form of Japanese ritual suicide by disembowelment. It was originally reserved for samurai, but was also practiced by other Japanese people later on to restore honor for themselves or for their family. *Major Tom lost control*—lyrics from the popular song "Space Oddity" by David Bowie (1969).

"Wasteland of Poetry": *Dante Alighieri* (c. 1265 – 1321)—Italian poet of the Late Middle Ages. His *Divine Comedy*, originally called *Comedìa* and later christened *Divina* by Boccaccio, is widely considered the greatest literary work composed in the Italian language and a masterpiece of world literature. *Morgue and other Poems*—Gotfried's 1912 collection of poems. *Benn Gotfried* (1886 –1956)—a German poet and essayist, a laid-off military doctor who in 1912 turned to pathology, where he dissected over 200 bodies between October 1912 and November 1913 in Berlin. Many of his literary works reflect his time as a pathologist. Benn began his literary career as a poet when he published a booklet entitled *Morgue and other Poems* (1912), containing expressionist poems dealing with the physical decay of flesh, blood, cancer, and death. *Álvaro de Campos* (1890 – ?) — one of the one of heteronyms of Portuguese poet Fernando Pessoa (1888-1935), a poet, writer, literary critic, translator, publisher and philosopher, described as one of the most significant literary figures of the 20th century and one of the greatest poets in the Portuguese language. He also wrote in and translated from English and French under four pseudonyms, widely known for his powerful and vivid writing style. *"The Tobacco Shop"* — a poem by Pessoa, published under his heteronym, Alvaro de Campos.

"Dartian Man": The italicized text was taken from the PLJUS forum.

"Demons in the Brothel": *"But something is happening and you don't know what it is, do you, Mr. Jones?"* — from Bob Dylan's "Ballad of a Thin Man" (1965).

## About the Author

Zvonko Karanović is a poet and fiction writer born in Niš, Serbia in 1959. His writing bears the influence of Beat literature, pop culture and Surrealism. As a writer of a distinctly urban sensibility, for many years he was an underground cult figure. His novel trilogy, *The Diary of Deserters*, is the first such project in 21st-century Serbian literature. Set in the period between April 1998 and October 5, 2000, the trilogy chronicles the lives of three young urban men who, fighting for their beliefs, attempt to live freely in an unfree land. The trilogy is dedicated to Serbia's "lost generation," those who, in the 1990s, either left the country, perished in the new Balkan wars, or suffered social marginalization due to their cosmopolitan worldview. All three novels received great attention. Karanović has received several Serbian literary awards for poetry: Laza Kostić, Biljana Jovanović, Kocić's Qill, Dušan Vasiljev, Ramond Serbica and an international fellowship for writers in 2011, awarded by the Heinrich Boll Foundation (Cologne, Germany), as well as others. His poems have been translated into sixteen languages: English, French, German, Spanish, Italian, Polish, Ukrainian, Greek, Hungarian, Bulgarian, Macedonian, Slovenian, Slovakian, Czech, Albanian and Arabic. He lives in Belgrade where he is the editor of the publishing house, PPM Enclave.

SELECTED PUBLICATIONS: Collections of poetry: *Blitzkrieg* (Niš: Samizdat, 1990), *Srebrni Surfer* (Niš: SKC, 1991; Belgrade: Home Books, 2001), *Mama melanholija* (Belgrade: Prosveta, 1996), *Extravaganza* (Niš: Gradina, 1997),

*Tamna magistrala* (Belgrade: Narodna Knjiga, 2001), *Neonski psi, izabrane pesme* (Belgrade: Home Books, 2001), *Svlačenje* (Kraljevo: Povelja, 2004), *Tamna magistrala,* selected poems in Croatia (Zagreb: Fraktura, 2008), *Box Set – sabrane pesme* (Belgrade: LOM, 2009), Барабаны и струны, магистраль и ночь in Ukraine (Lviv: Piramida, 2011), *Mesečari na izletu,* prose poems (Belgrade: LOM, 2012), *Kavezi* (Belgrade: LOM, 2013), *Burn, Baby, Burn – Selected Poems* in Austria (Klagenfurt: Drava Verlag, 2013), *Najbolje godine naših života – izbrane pesme 1991 – 2004* (Belgrade: LOM, 2014), Пепелашка во хромиран ковчег – selected poems in Macedonia (Skopje: Blesok, 2014), *Zlatno Doba* (Belgrade: LOM, 2015), *It Was Easy To Set the Snow On Fire – Selected Poems* in English, Transl. Ana Božićević (Los Angeles: Phoneme Media, 2016), *Iza Zapaljene Šume* (Belgrade: LOM, 2018), *The Best Years of Our Lives: Selected Poems* (Ljubljana: LUD Šerpa, 2017), and *The Best Years of Our Lives: Selected Poems* (Milano: Almutawassit, Palestine, 2018). Novels: *Više od nule* (Niš: Zograf, 2004, 2005; Belgrade: Laguna, 2006), *Četiri zida i grad* (Belgrade: Laguna, 2006, 2008), *Tri slike pobede* (Belgrade: Laguna, 2009, 2010); Četiri zida i grad was translated into Ukranian, Чотири стини и мисто (Kiev, FAKT, 2009) as well as *Tri slike pobede –* Три картини перемоги, (Kiev, Комора, 2016; 2017). Anthologies: most significantly, in the US, *New European Poets* (Minneapolis: Graywolf Press, 2008), *Zvezde su lepe, ali nemam kad da ih gledam – Antologija srpske urbane poezije* (Belgrade: B92, 2009), *Iz muzeja šumova – Antologija novije srpske poezije* in Croatia (Zagreb: VBZ, 2009), *The Ticket/ Ulaznica, a Panorama of Contemporary Serbian Poetry,* in Austria (Klagenfurt: Drava Verlag, 2011).

# About the Translator

Dr. Biljana D. Obradović, is a Serbian-American poet, critic and translator. She has lived and studied in Greece, India, the U.S., and the ex-Yugoslavia. She has a B.A. in English Language and Literature from Belgrade University, an M.F.A. in Creative Writing from Virginia Commonwealth University, and a Ph.D. in English from the University of Nebraska, Lincoln. She writes in English. Her first collection of poems, *Frozen Embraces*, a bilingual edition (Center of Emigrants from Serbia, 1997, 2000), won the Rastko Petrović Award for the Best Book of 1998. Her second collection, *Le Riche Monde*, appeared in a bilingual edition (Raška Škola, 1999). Her third collection, *Little Disruptions* (Niš Cultural Center, 2012), was also a bilingual edition, while her fourth, *Incognito*, only appeared in English (WordTech Press, 2017). Her poems also appear in *Three Poets in New Orleans* (Xavier Review Press, 2000). She has also published Serbian translations of John Gery's *American Ghosts: Selected Poems* (1999), Stanley Kunitz's, *The Long Boat* (2007), *Fives: Fifty Poems by Serbian and American Poets,* as editor and translator (2002), Patrizia de Rachewiltz's *Dear Friends* (2012), Bruce Weigl's *What Saves Us* (2013), Niyi Osundare's *The Tongue Is a Pink Fire* (2015), and English translations from Serbian of Bratislav Milanović's, *Doors in a Meadow (*2011). She is the main translator and co-editor with Dubravka Djurić of *Cat Painters: An Anthology of Contemporary Serbian Poetry* (with a preface by Charles Bernstein, Diálogos, 2016). She is also the editor of Philip Dacey's *Heavenly Muse: Essays on Poetry*

(Diálogos, 2020). She reviews books for *World Literature Today* and *Serbian Studies*. Her poems have been translated into Serbian, Italian, Arabic, and Korean. She is the recipient of the NCF Award for Excellence in Research for 2015 at Xavier University of Louisiana, in New Orleans where she is Professor of English. She lives in New Orleans with her husband, the poet, John Gery, and their son Petar.

Zvonko Karanović and Biljana D. Obradović met in May 2012 in Belgrade at the Serbian Writers Association where she was visiting in order to begin working on her sabbatical project, co-editing, *Cat Painters: An Anthology of Contemporary Serbian Poetry* (Diálogos, 2016), as he was one of the writers in the anthology. She has published translated into English, one of his poems and interviewed him for *World Literature Today*.

## About the Artist

Simon Kastelic was born in Postojna, Slovenia in 1977. He graduated in 2005 in Painting at the Accademia di Belle Arti in Venice. Thereafter, he received a Master's Degree in Painting at the Academy of Fine Arts in Ljubljana. So far, he has exhibited his work at joint exhibitions in Italy, Austria, the United Kingdom, France and Slovakia and has had thirty solo exhibitions. He has received numerous awards. His work is based on digital realism and media image, even though he remains a classical painter, bound by colors and canvas. In addition to painting, he also works with video, computer graphics, digital photography, illustrations and installations. He is a Professor at the College of Stone Design and Photography, at the Higher Vocational College in Sežana, Slovenia.

**DIÁLOGOS
BOOKS**
New Orleans
Diálogosbooks.com

CPSIA information can be obtained
at www.ICGtesting.com
Printed in the USA
FSHW011113211021
85618FS